Be Encouraged
By
Black Men

Edited by: Jerrica Stovall

Other Titles by Jerrica Stovall:

*Be Encouraged: 20 Testaments of God's Faith,
Love, and Loyalty*

Be Encouraged by Black Men

This book is dedicated to my dad, Thomas Washington

-Love, Jerrica

CONTENTS

ACKNOWLEDGMENTS

Many thanks to everyone who contributed to Be Encouraged by Black Men in one way or another. It's wild to have so many people support God's plans for me. I am continually humbled.

Sydney Stovall

Nathaniel Stovall

Vnai Ashe

Jessica Sanchez-Williams

Jillian Clark

Abigail Bradley-Tyler

Foreword

"Name one place where a black man can find mental rest?" he asked. "It's not the police, it's not our neighborhoods and it's definitely not white people's neighborhoods. It's no place where we can shut down." David Banner, Hip-Hop Artist, Actor, and Activist (NBC News, 2017)

The concept of Black Men discussing their stories, particularly narratives rooted in life-changing experiences and past traumas, while revealing emotional vulnerabilities typically hidden from the rest of the world, remains a relatively novel one. This is the case despite recent progress being made to bring these stories to the forefront via movements in various mental health and wellness spaces, to normalize therapy and greater sharing amongst Black Men of such narratives. As an entertainment medium, often dominated by Black Men, Hip-Hop music has also found itself as a platform and catalyst for Black Men to increasingly share the moments and experiences that have shaped who they are. However, the distance between DMX rapping about overcoming his demons in "Slippin'" in 1998 and Kid Cudi tweeting about depression and suicidal ideation shortly before entering rehab in 2016 is 18 long years. In that span of time, my Black, queer, southern conscious, and evolution from a boy to a man was constantly shaped by what I experienced in my own life. Additionally, there were the narratives I consumed about others, most notably musical artists as a life-long fan of the artform. Yet, how transformative might it have been to be exposed to stories that allowed me to see myself, my struggles, my experiences, and my triumphs put on display via Black Men. Particularly, Black Men who lived through similar life moments and were now able to discuss the role of faith, support, love, therapy, amongst other resources, in overcoming the moments that could have decimated them?

Unfortunately, as art often imitates life, there was a dearth of these real and open conversations in my life until I reached my late 20s.

Although I spent the majority of my college years in a historically Black fraternity, wherein my Brothers and I identified many of our similarities, even some of our traumas, what we did not discuss was the magnitude of those experiences on who we were and their impact on who we were becoming, for better or worse. We simply did not have the tools and wherewithal to know how transformative it could be, to heal as a collective. And, the fact that we could help heal one another and ourselves simply by talking more, remains both awe-inspiring and aspirational.

This is the unique space in which *Be Encouraged by Black Men* sits. During a time marked by social unrest, significant public health and environmental threats, and a constantly evaporating sense of common decency, integrity, and care for others, this text reminds us of what can happen when we understand the power of a story to heal. Moreover, it provides a space that is cathartic for the authors and readers of this volume. In the stories that lie ahead, you will read about how Black Men overcame the deaths of loved ones, their own near-death experiences, addiction, abuse, and faith when it literally felt like they were losing it all. You will even encounter Black

Men who navigated the potential minefield of honoring themselves fully through the process of articulating their sexual identity. And yet, on the next page, and in the next chapter, you will find another story with a Black man baring his soul and revealing his heart during times of chaos, confusion, and doubt, while on the verge of restoration, triumph, and healing. Much like the space many of us are aspiring to, particularly given the present.

Be Encouraged by Black Men speaks to the power inherent in the narratives of Black Men. Narratives that have often been discarded for more superficial representations of Black Men that center on emotional erasure and toxic actions and beliefs. Black Men are more than that. Although we are being encouraged to be more open with our feelings, that does not mean that we have lacked them our entire lives. We simply needed the encouragement, validation, and platform to share these aspects of ourselves that we often felt the world force into hiding for our own survival. However, we must realize that now, more than ever, our ability to survive and thrive is not predicated by how much we can bear, but rather on our ability to intentionally bare our souls in the process of seeking the healing we need and deserve. The more we have access to books and other artforms centering our narratives as told by us, the greater our chances of receiving that healing and becoming better because of it.

In providing this warm, safe space for Black Men to convene and share, as she has done for Black women and Women of Color in her previous installment, Jerrica Stovall has once again affirmed two undeniable laws of the universe, the Black Woman plays a crucial role in our collective healing, and Faith is transformative.

As a Black man and a dear friend, I cannot thank you enough for having the heart and vision to conceptualize and see this project through. It is because of your attention and care to the needs of others to heal, that so many of us are still here today. Moreover, I hope that you possess zero doubt that this text, that has been carefully co-constructed with 19 dynamic Black Men, will heal hearts, save lives, and shift paradigms and perspectives for the better. In identifying the role of faith and acknowledging the power of shared testimonies, you solidify the need to rely on, and believe in a higher power calling upon us all to live our best life and be our best self; not for our own glory but for the God In each of us to shine brightly, illuminating the path to our destinies.

Suffice it to say, I am encouraged, and you will be too, with each turn of the page. In solidarity for Black lives and in pursuit of vibrant   Black futures,

Brandon D. Brown, M.S.Ed.

Be Encouraged by Black Men

1

A Heavy Hit to an Almost Empty Soul

Sadandre' Jackson
Greensboro, NC

I used to think that we spend our entire lives just gathering guests for our own funeral. We laugh when it's time to laugh, and hopefully cry when it's time to cry. It was easy to understand that life is full of extremities and it's our free will to decide which one or ones we choose to partake in. Yet, this was one of the most difficult times of my life.

When I moved out of my hometown to attend college, I also moved away from the idea that the traditional aspects of Christianity are something I wanted to believe and take part in. The idea of having to go to church every Sunday just to prove that I was a Christian really didn't sit well with me because I knew the relationship I had with God and it was full of mini conversations throughout the day. Over the course of two years I gradually lost my faith in happiness, in hope, and any other abstract idea that felt too far-fetched to physically grasp and experience. I spent hours at night asking myself reflection questions that took me a year to find answers, despite my burning desire to have an immediate remedy be presented to me in some sort of fashion. I would sit and ask myself questions like, "Why is happiness something that we are taught to believe in when we are young and vulnerable, and it's really an intangible, empty, and hopeless figment of our imagination? What is the point of believing in love at first sight when it is really just a magnetism of energies, as that is how human nature works?" I felt very strongly about challenging the common concepts of happiness and love. I went on with life carrying this weight and operating in a spirit of entitlement that made me relish in the powers of my own intelligence and earthly righteousness.

During October of this entitlement wave is when my biggest reality check came. It was my birthday week and I had just moved into a new crib so I was excited to have my friends over to turn up. This is also the week of homecoming so there were hype events happening everyday including some that I participated in. I had successfully planned a huge team performance event for that same week and I just knew it would be the highlight. After the team performance was over, I left to head to the mall to buy birthday presents for my other Libra friends. I hopped in the car like it was just another day. Music blasting, my favorite sunglasses on, a cold Pepsi in the cup holder, roads clear and ready for me to cruise on through so I could get to the mall. Not even 10 minutes into the car ride my car was smacked against another car, spinning out in the middle of the street eventually coming to a halt right before hitting a light pole. With my head leaning against the window all I could mutter was the word "Jesus." I sat there in pain listening to what sounded like silence inside my head and muffled chaos outside of the car. "Jesus." "Jesus." I could only repeat what was instinctual in a time of terror. My car had been totaled. I managed to stumble out of the car and ran to the other car to make sure they were okay. After all was said and done the first thing I did when I entered my apartment was cry.

Now my hours of nightly reflection turned to focusing on why this has happened to me. My questions now became, "God what are you trying to teach me? Where is the answer code or the cheat sheet because I just know you are making this harder than it needs to be? You know I am smart and you know that I try to be obedient to your word, so God what is going on here because I am sitting in classes everyday learning difficult topics like differential calculus, but I can't even see what you are putting in front of me? And to add extra frustration to the situation this just had to happen during my birthday week when I am supposed to be celebrating another year of life on this very earth that you chose to put me on?" Then God told me to be still and listen. Put everything down, turn everything off and listen to me. God said you are flourishing in this new city that I placed you in as you make friends, live on your own, win these awards and accolades in school, and make a name for yourself in this beautiful community. What you failed to realize is you are doing all of this without me. This is not the agreement we had so I am holding you responsible for your actions as you are stripped of happiness, joy, a car, money, confidence and your smile.

There is a reason why in that split moment after the car accident I didn't repeat the faith-challenging questions I had just spent so much time and mental energy thinking on during the same week. I didn't repeat my name or another human's name. All I could call on was the name of Jesus, my joy giver and way maker. I believe God had to physically shake me to get my attention. I could not feel the ground underneath me, the sky seemed like it was spinning and I could not hear clearly. I had to be rebalanced. My core had to be shaken, hit, and swirled around. What happened to me in the accident also literally happened to my spirit. God took everything away from me that I was comfortable with and taking advantage of and told me to listen to him.

I sat in church the following week and two worship songs shook me to my core so hard that I couldn't even sing the words from my seat, all I could do was kneel and cry out to God. Over and over again, I repeated, "Take everything away from me God because all I want is you." Those are the words that came from my heart and this is still my prayer today. I failed to remember that we exist because someone loved us first. He loved us so much that He proved it by trading his life for our real happiness and love.

Looking back on this time, I do not think it was coincidental that this happened around the time of my birthday. I now realize how selfish of me it was to be extremely upset that this happened to me during a time of celebrating my birth because that car ride could have been the last thing I did as a living and breathing human. God's grace and mercy spared my life that day and allowed me to see another rotation around the sun.

Be Encouraged by Black Men

I had a conversation with myself and realized where one of my greatest faults existed. I told myself "teachability is the concept that you have completely ignored. If you want to grow, you have to remain teachable. If you do not like the crop you are reaping, check the seed you are sowing." Fast forward three years later and I am feeling stronger than I have ever felt. God has placed me in a new city and state with an amazing career and a new school program. I have a car, I have been reaping financial blessings left and right, I have a fitness and health journey that I am on, a beautiful support system of family and friends, and most importantly I have faith in faith again. The moral of my testimony is that humility and self-righteousness cannot exist within the same space. God is a God of love, of serenity and of confidence. When we put our own entitled ego and flesh into the equation, we lessen the space that we are giving Him to work in us. God did not put us on this green earth to fake it until we make it. He expects us to operate in a spirit of teachability because that spirit strictly requires a humility as a prerequisite. As a disciple and a giver, I am blessed to be on this spiritual journey that was crafted just for me. Here is an excerpt from a poem I wrote during the resolution of my egotistical chaos:

Today I am a thought

A thought of existence

A thought in a world of a million ideas and spaces to be free

Word clouds exist around me

Waiting to be filled by my imagination

Today I want to begin again

Be Encouraged by Black Men

Exist in the evergreen nature of sun and shiny purities

I choose to suspend my expectations

To arrest my disbelief of happiness

This is not easy

I am not from a bubble of merriment

I am from letting my inner me be my biggest enemy

I am from the silent screams that are only loud enough for my heart

to hear

I am from long nights of humbling prayers

I am from the emotional slumps that deprive the lives of hope and

faith in my life

Yet today I am a thought

I choose to give thanks

I can blink

I can smell

I can smile at my heart and give thanks to it for beating today

I choose to wrap my soul like a blanket in the warmth of earth's

energies

For I have not healed myself but I have been healed

I deliver truth from my tongue to the air

I decree an exchange of fear for joy

I embrace the sensitivity that pounds through my chest and drips

from my eyes

I am free

I use the pain of yesterday as the foundation for a thought today so

that tomorrow can be reality

As wind is to fire

Be Encouraged by Black Men

Action is my heart's desire
Today I am about me
Sprouting to be
Seeding the curiosity
Picking the weeds
Feeding the confidence of today
Shining the creativity
Buffing the authenticity
Today I am a thought
Will I be my own reality?

2

Hidden Blessings During COVID-19
Aerial Hall Jr.
Tampa, FL

When 2020 first began, I just knew that I was going to make this year something special. I had every intention on reaching every goal that I set. I figured I had everything planned out, but God had other plans. Plans that would force me to refocus and to be grateful of every blessing brought my way.

As a Graduate Student, one of my tasks was to secure a summer internship. Traditionally, all students interview in January/February and the first round of acceptance letters go out shortly after. I had my sights set on an internship that would allow me to travel to a different state and would offer pay + housing. I had two different rounds of interviews. One interview was a recorded session and the other was a live session with a representative from the institution. After these two interviews I was extended an offer. Things were going according to plan.

My personal life also saw a positive start in 2020. I started pursuing a dream of mine to become a professional wrestler. I have been a fan of the art since middle school and I decided to try it. I started training in February and I was making great progress through my early days. My coaches told me that I was learning fast and that my first match would be later in the year. Life was going great. I secured my summer internship and I was chasing a dream. I felt unstoppable. Then, March came around and we were introduced to a global pandemic.

When I first heard of COVID-19, I immediately disregarded it. Like Ebola, I selfishly considered it to be another sickness that would not have any affect on me. Then, everything started to change drastically and out of nowhere. I was used to my set schedule of going to work in the morning, class in the afternoon, then practice in the evening. Before I knew it, my entire schedule shifted and I was suddenly instructed to work from home and attend classes virtually.

My wrestling dreams also came to a sudden stop. I could no longer go to wrestling practice because the trainings were put on hold, and during one of the last days I had a practice, I reaggravated a previous shoulder injury.

At first, I thought it would be something that I could work through. All of a sudden, I couldn't lift my arm at all. I knew I needed to get medical help.

After a few trips to the doctor, I found out that I would need shoulder surgery to repair damaged ligaments and remove bone fragments. Unfortunately, due to COVID-19, I was not able to get surgery immediately due to the surgery center closing down for all of March and all of April. I had to be waitlisted until the surgery center reopened.

Over the span of 4 weeks, my entire life had been turned upside down. I felt defeated. What started out to be a great year, became one of the most challenging. I spent every day hoping that COVID-19 would just disappear and I could return to chasing my dreams and accomplishing my goals. I received monthly updates from my summer internship with hopes that I would still be able to go in June. As Summer got closer, COVID-19 showed me that it wasn't going anywhere. Inevitably, my Summer internship was cancelled and I found myself jobless for the Summer. I was distraught…but God.

Once summer arrived, things began to reopen and blessings started to pour in. Starting off, I was able to find another internship. Initially, the internship was not supposed to be paid, but my supervisor informed me a week before I began that I would be able to get paid. This same internship allowed me to do work with communities that I hold close to my heart and granted me the opportunity to begin new initiatives that the office can continue even after my appointment ended. The internship would be based in Tampa, so I was not able to travel like I wanted. However, I was allowed to work from home which proved to be another hidden blessing.

Another area where God blessed me would be for my shoulder surgery. Initially, I was slated to have the surgery in May, but due to my travel plans of visiting my Dad for a week, the hospital informed me that I could not have the surgery in May and that I would need to reschedule. Initially, I was upset, but then found out that my surgery cost total over $2,000 and I did not have the money to pay for it at that time. My surgery being postponed for one month allowed me to find a way to save enough. I was able to set a date for my surgery in June.

I prayed to God that He would provide and He provided. I had not even started my internship yet, but God found a way for me to get enough money just days before the procedure so that I could pay for the operation. Like they say, He may not be there when you call Him, but He's always on time! On top of that, I needed to be at home as much as possible during recovery. Me having my internship be a work-from-home internship allowed me to recover all while working remote. Once again, God took care of me through challenging times.

Here I am now, getting prepared for the Fall. I am two months into my recovery and my physical therapist says that I am healing well. I completed my internship and started my other job again for the Fall Semester. I am now preparing for classes to begin and looking forward towhat the rest of 2020 has to bring.

In retrospect, I realize that I started this year trying to control my future. I thought that I had it all figured out, but God had a change of plans. He showed me that I always need Him. I needed to be humbled, and I am grateful for the experience. He changed my path, but led me to a greater destination. This experience has reminded me to always look to God and to remain thankful.

3
More Than Enough
Tino Johnson
Athens, GA

I grew up in a small rural community in Southeast Georgia. We did not have much, but it was always enough. I know that sounds like a line straight out of a made for television movie, but those lines are generally crafted from truths.

I often recall memories from my childhood, most fond but some not so fond. Some of the memories date as far back to the age of three which includes things like missing snack time in Head Start because I enjoyed naptime more. Honestly, a lot of my early memories were from school, because I excelled as a student which made the teachers notice me. Later memories, include the other children living in Trash Circle, the public housing where we lived during my earliest childhood years, not wanting to play with me…but that was cool though since I had no problem playing by myself. To this day, I still consider myself the coolest person I know.

Another memory centers around visiting with my great grandparents, both of whom were disabled. My great grandfather lost his leg to gangrene when I was very young and my great grandmother lost her sight before I was born. It was fun helping them with things around the house, and errands, but not so fun receiving the butterscotch hard candy from my grandfather as a "treat." The interesting thing about most of my childhood memories is that I don't remember the date, day, or time of many of them. However, the most vivid memory happened the morning of January 19, 1985.

If you grew up as a young child in the 80's you probably remember Saturday morning cartoons. Like my son today, I was always an early riser. The house I grew up in only had one television, and Saturday mornings between 9:00 and 11:00 were dedicated to NBC cartoons. Don't ask me why I liked the Smurfs so much, I just did. January 19, 1985 was a Saturday. I awoke early, as I always did, and journeyed into the living room. To my surprise, a stranger with wild hair slept in the very spot where I had watched cartoons every Saturday. As I stood surprised, I recalled a conversation with my mother about a visitor who was to be my little brother. But this stranger was not him. No "she" was "too big" to be my "little brother." Somewhat alarmed, but quietly, I walked to my mother's room to notify her that a stranger was in our home. Unalarmed, my mother told me "baby that's your mother."

This is where my testimony and family tree gets a little confusing, but, let's be honest, what black family tree isn't confusing?

I was born in Boston, Massachusetts on September 7, 1979 to a 19 year old young woman. My father, as my birth certificate shows, is unknown. However, I have a name and I have heard a voice, which is more than enough for me. Shortly after my birth, my mother (on the actual family tree, she is my great aunt, my maternal grandmother's sister) traveled to Boston and brought me home to Southeast Georgia. For about a year and a half she raised me as her own. It was just the two of us. I was too young to remember when my cousin arrived but he was only 15 days younger than me. Though we knew we were cousins, we were raised by my mother, his grandmother, like brothers. My cousin's mother was murdered and his father was not comfortable raising his son alone. So, for about four years it was just the three of us. Then in 1985, when I was five years old, my understanding of family was fractured and pieced back together.

I remember being confused, yet unmoved by my mom's confession about our new houseguest. (For the purpose of clearing confusion my mom will be played by my great aunt who raised me, and my mother will be the lady who gave birth to me.) My only question was, "Can she find another place to sleep? I would like to watch Saturday morning cartoons." Laugh out loud, I do not recall watching cartoons that morning. I also do not recall having much of a conversation or interaction with my mother. That statement has remained true for 35 years now. My mother lived with us for about 2 years before vanishing. She returned when I was 12 and has been connected to me in some form ever since.

At the age of 17 I was working at a summer camp in the north Georgia mountains when my mom called to ask, "Guess what?" The answer, "your mother is pregnant." I remember asking my mom why people continued to have children they would never take care of. And no, my mother did not raise my sister either. If you haven't lost count yet, then there were 5. Our three bedroom, one television home was now my mom, myself, my younger cousin, my little brother, and my little sister.

As the oldest, I always felt responsible for making sure things were taken care of. I remember being in my senior year of high school, college decision time was quickly approaching, and my mom was continuously sick. I could not leave home. If I did, who would pay the bills? Who would make sure my siblings stayed out of trouble? Believe me, back then, their best friends were trouble. So, I stayed home after high school and attended the local Junior College. After two years it was time to move on, but I remained a third year and decided to take Physics before transferring to the University of Georgia.

My mom was still sick, but I knew that I could not remain at home. There was nothing for me in our small town. I remember how proud and happy she was the day I left home for Athens, GA to obtain my first college degree. I brought her checkbook with me and I paid the bills, monthly, from 4 hours away. Additionally, I knew the only way to pay for my education at the University of Georgia, was to get a job and make as much money as I could while maintaining my scholarships. I waited table at Applebee's, which could be a separate testimony.

It was my second semester at Georgia and I was working the morning shift, prepping for opening, when my cell phone rang. My little brother was crying on the other end and told me that my mom had died. I was angry to not know that she was sick again. He told me she wasn't and that she had been with friends the day before. They went fishing, ate great food, and had a wonderful time. She laid down and never awoke. My little sister found her and could not wake her. I was devastated.

My relationship with God has always been a private one that I don't often share with others. However, I will tell you, God has always been with me and has surrounded me with angels. My mom was an angel. She was, and will always be my biggest fan. Even though she is no longer physically here on earth, I hear her voice often. She still guides me. Sometimes I thought her kindness was too much. She was the type of woman to help anyone and would give her last dime to a stranger regardless of what her needs were. She sacrificed so much to make sure my siblings and I had a chance.

God's plan is unknown but should always be trusted. Walking in the faith that (S)He has your best interest and favor in all that happens, is peace.

Today, I am a successful professional with a long career in higher education. I am married to a Ph.D. in higher education and have two beautiful children (one of which is named after my mom). If my story were written any other way, I would not be who or where I am today. I am thankful to my mother for being who she is and I am grateful to my mom for her sacrifice. Whether they were the source of joy or pain, God strategically used both of them to help me and so many others.

4

From a Boy to a Man

London B. Brown
Tampa, FL

As I began to take this journey of deep thought and meditation about my testimony I had some doubt. I expressed to a friend, "I do not have a testimony." My friend replied, "Everyone's testimony is different," and who would have known those simple words would resonate with me for the next few months. I always thought of any testimony I had as not big enough, thinking that it had to be this near death out of body experience and return to reality type of story. Man was I wrong. It dawned on me that my testimony is not a one size fits all but a right sized fit made just for me. As a reference throughout my testimony, reflect on 1 Corinthians 13:11.When I finally finished searching, meditating, and praying about what my testimony was, I could not wait to share it in hopes that it would resonate with just one person.

I always dreamed of being a husband and a father one day. I wanted to be a married man, a husband to one wife and show her how great of a husband I am. What I was not prepared for was the work that goes into a successful marriage. I had my own views and examples of what marriage looked like and I would later learn what worked for others did not work for us. My wife and I were married in August of 2012. This was all after a failed attempt to complete college, wasted money, a broken jaw, and enlistment into the U.S. military.

Marriage is beautiful, but it takes work. After my wife and I were married at 25 years old, I still had a boyish mindset. I'll give an example: playing basketball was a major part of my life and I had to play it as often as I could to meet my fix. That meant after work, weekends, and even during promised family time. I just had to have it. It was close to an addiction, but really just a very close affinity for the sport. It was not until my wife confronted me about how I was spending my time and how immature it was for me to dedicate so much time to something that was not meeting the needs of our family, that I realized it was time for growth. A stepping stone in learning of what it took to be a husband. That meant being present, and not selfish. This was a relatively easy lesson in graduating from a boy to a man. Alas, my transformation was not complete.

Next, in my transition to a becoming a man, I encountered my toughest hurdle. My wife and I were well into our second to third year of marriage and our families were about eleven hours away from us. This was a time where I was learning to leave and cleave unto my wife. Often times I sought advice from others who were not qualified, complained to my mother, or put my parents' needs before the needs of my queen. I learned rather slowly that this was the quickest way to hinder growth. For example, my parents wanted to discipline our oldest son the same way I had been disciplined growing up. Initially, I had given the blessing to my parents to do what they needed to do in order for my oldest son to listen. In a perfect world that would have been fine but in an attempt set parameters and not really have the H.A.M (hard as a mothe*****) attitude, I later learned that discussions such as this one need to happen between a husband and wife. This was a decision that should not have been made alone, but instead, always consulting each other when it comes to very serious decisions.

Another point of reference during this tumultuous period was not demanding respect for my wife. Instances would include mean remarks, yelling, and unfair practices that were done by some of my family. The problem with it was not that I was unaware, but for a long time I did nothing to correct it. This went on for a few years until I finally went through counseling, and more importantly listened to my wife's feelings. After much prayer, supplication, and conjuring up some bravery, I was able to confront my family and champion for my wife. Demanding equal respect for my wife was important to our extended families, but more important to our growth as a couple. Even in this moment in time it was instrumental in my individual growth. Although, tremendous leaps and bounds had taken place, I still had not fully become a man.

Lastly, listening has been one of the biggest tasks I have yet to overcome. I am ashamed to say that I have not mastered listening, but I have graduated to a better degree. I would say from year one of marriage to year seven, I struggled with listening to what was being said to me from my spouse. I focused more on responding with a rebuttal and the tone of what was being said. Listening was hard for me because I wanted to be correct in every argument, conversation, and idea that we engaged in. I wanted to be the man who was right because I was in charge and because I was the stronger vessel. Often times arguments would go nowhere because I would not just slow down and listen. It was not until counseling, prayer, and meditation on wanting to grow with my spouse that I was able to finally hear her out. I knew at that moment when I took time and squinted with my ears and not with my mouth, resolutions and progression could move forward. As my wife and I have entered year 8 of our commitment to Christ, we have seen more resolution than ever before.

My testimony came in the form of growth. The type of growth that you requires commitment, a strong spouse, prayer and meditation. I did not see this coming but Lawd am I thankful for it. As my friend says, "Everyone's testimony is different."

5

God's Timing is Perfect

Jaret Lloyd
Upper Marlboro, MD

On June 6, 2019 while heading home after meeting some friends for happy hour, I was struck by a drunk driver causing me to lose control of my vehicle and crash through a guard rail on the right side of the highway. By the time my vehicle came to a complete stop I had landed into a ditch on the side of the highway, facing the opposite way of traffic with my vehicle now sitting on two wheels. I was completely blindsided by the driver that struck me so when my vehicle came to a complete stop, I was in total shock of what just happened. After the initial shock wore off, I began to look around to assess the damages. I quickly take a glance into my rearview mirror to see if I received any injuries to my face or head and thankfully not a scratch was found. I then took a sigh of relief and noticed my two front teeth were chipped. I thought to myself "That's not too bad," if that is the extent of my injuries. I then looked around my vehicle and noticed all the airbags were deployed, covering up all the windows in my small 2011 Chevy Camaro. Now anxiety begins to set in because my vehicle is sitting on a slanted hill and I am blinded from being able to see anything outside of my vehicle. I begin to think, the vehicle may roll over, fuel may be leaking, or there could be other vehicles involved. I now determine that I need to get out of the vehicle as soon as possible.

First, I attempt to open my passenger side door, but it was jammed shut. I did not attempt to open my driver side door for fear that the vehicle may roll over. Next, I decide that I needed to try and kick out the windows to get out. I must have thought I was Chuck Norris or something. I began to prop my legs up to try and kick out the front windshield and I notice that I could not move my left leg. Moments later, I hear a voice yell out "Are you ok in there?" I yelled back "Yes, but I believe my leg is broken and my door is jammed shut." This God-sent good Samaritan then proceeds to prop open my passenger side door and helps me climb out of the vehicle. Once I make it out of the vehicle, I lay flat on the ground just thankful that I made it out safely. At this point, the adrenalin starts to subside, and my left leg is now in excruciating pain. A few more good Samaritans come to the scene to try and comfort me and let me know that the ambulance is on its way. I look up at my 2011 Chevrolet Camaro and it looks completely unrecognizable. There is no doubt that God's presence was there protecting me. Moments later, the paramedics arrive to haul me off into the ambulance with a gurney and transport me to the hospital. This was my first time in an ambulance, and it was not a fun ride at all. The ambulance driver was swerving left to right weaving through traffic and at this point my leg was throbbing because of the pressure. Surprisingly, a calm spirit falls over me and

I believe it was God letting me know that everything was going to be alright. Once I arrived at the hospital, the doctors ran a CAT scan on me to ensure that I did not have any head trauma. Thankfully, no head trauma was detected. After running a series of x-rays, doctors determined that my left femur bone had snapped due to the impact of the collision. The doctor advised me that I would need to be rushed into surgery in matter of a few hours and that they would need to insert a medal rod into my femur bone to connect it back together. Everything was happening so fast. I have always been a healthy person, so I have never had any surgery or even had to spend a night in a hospital for any illness or injury. I was just at happy hour enjoying life with friends and in a matter of hours I had to undergo a major surgery that could alter my leg for the rest of my life.

However, I believe that God has a purpose for every tragedy that we go through. Many times, God will allow you to experience the tragedy to prepare you for the triumph. Hours later, I awoke from having a successful surgery and the doctor advised that I would have a full recovery after completing months of physical therapy. My parents decided to take me down to Chesapeake, VA with them to completely heal.

Now this may seem like just a tragic story, but it is a testimony of God's perfect timing for several different reasons. Reason One: Just 20 minutes prior to the accident occurring I had just dropped off one of my friends at their residence. Had the accident occurred sooner there could have been multiple people injured from the collision. Reason Two: At the beginning of 2019, I prayed to God to allow me the opportunity to purchase my first home.

When I was younger, I made a lot of poor financial decisions that led to me having poor credit. Starting in 2018, I began to work diligently at paying debt off and boosting my credit score. In 2019 I begin to try and pre-qualify for home loans, but I still was not quite meeting the criteria to qualify. As God would have it, my vehicle had been claimed a total loss from the accident. Not only did the insurance company cut me a check to pay my vehicle off, but they also paid me an additional $3,000 based off the assessed value of the vehicle. Now that my vehicle was paid off this significantly boosted my credit score and decreased my debt to income ratio allowing me to now qualify for the home loan.

Weeks later, I spoke with my lender at Navy Federal Credit Union and they advised that I now qualified for a VA Home Loan for $400,000. What a blessing! Shortly after qualifying for the home loan I took a trip back to Maryland with my father and to look at some potential homes. We ended up stumbling across a new construction townhome complex in Upper Marlboro, MD. The sales consultant for the complex took us on a tour of the model and it was perfect. It had everything I was looking for in a home and the price was within the budget that I was looking to stay in. The next day we came back, and I purchased the lot for my new home! I never imagined that my first home would be built from the ground up.

Reason Three: Everything seemed to be going great now. Physical therapy was going well, and I was beginning to learn how to walk again with crutches. However, I now had a dilemma because I no longer had a vehicle and I needed transportation to eventually get back to work. If I did purchase another vehicle, that could potentially disqualify me from my home loan being that my house was a new build, and I had to wait 6 months until my house was complete before I could close on the loan.

When God has a plan for you, He will always make a way. I reached out to my lender at Navy Federal Credit Union and explained my situation. To my surprise, she advised me that based on my improved credit they would be able to finance a new vehicle for me up to $35,000 without it affecting my home loan. Look at God!! Days later, I went to Carmax and used the $3000 from the insurance company to put a down payment a 2015 Jeep Grand Cherokee.

In just a matter of months after this tragic accident, God blessed me with a purchase of a new house and a new vehicle. Just when I thought God was finished, he went above and beyond what I asked of Him. Reason Four: While rehabbing my leg down in Chesapeake, VA I was out of work on short-term disability. After being out on short-term disability for about eight weeks, I received a call from my employer asking If I would be returning to work soon. At this time, I was barely getting around on crutches so it would be difficult for me to get to and from my job which was located downtown Washington D.C. I explained to my employer that I needed more time to heal before I could get back to work. I still had about 8 weeks left of short-term disability insurance to claim so there was no reason to rush. My employer did not like that I would not be returning soon and advised that if I could not return soon, I could possibly be replaced. You may be thinking "Can an employer actually do that?" At the time I was working as a government contractor and as a contractor you are considered an "at-will" employee, which basically means your employer does not need good cause to fire you.

However, God is faithful and will supply all your needs. Days later, I received a random call from a recruiter with Science Applications International Corporation (SAIC), a premier fortune 500 technology company, looking to fill an I.T. position at the Pentagon. The position offered a 20K raise in pay, excellent benefits and an opportunity to work in the world's largest office. The recruiter expressed that they found my resume online and felt that it was a perfect match for the position. After speaking in further detail about the position, we both agreed it would be a good fit and an interview was scheduled with the program manager later that week. The interview went extremely well, and I was offered the position!

Psalm 23:5 states, "Thou preparest a table before me in the presence of mine enemies: thou anointest my head with oil; my cup runneth over." While I thought I was experiencing the biggest tragedy I had ever faced, God was preparing me for my life's biggest triumph. Sometimes God will sit you down and humble you for you to realize that He is always in control. Ephesians 2:10 says, "For we are his workman His workmanship created in Christ Jesus for good works, which God prepared beforehand, that we should walk in them." The accident could have easily taken me out, but God had a higher purpose for me to fulfill and I'm thankful that he continues to bless me with the tools to fulfill it.

6

Hard Point

Dante Jones
Atlanta, GA

I remember it like it was yesterday. It was about 7am CST and I got a call from my wife, "Hey babe, are you up?" she asked. "Yeah babe, I'm up what's going on?" "Oh nothing, in the hospital our baby girl is on her way." I jump out of the bed and hit the road to Atlanta from Mississippi. Overcome with emotion all I could think was I am NOT going to miss my daughter coming into this world. I speed to Atlanta to be by her side and welcome our baby girl into the world. My wife was in Atlanta because a job of hers had fallen through in Mississippi, and she was able to find work in Atlanta and be with her mom, sister, and grandmother. We traveled back and forth for a year and a half, mostly while she was pregnant and after our daughter was born. Now I know you might be thinking "why is this pregnant woman driving back and forth?" It was important to her that we were in our own space instead of a shared space when possible. On top of being pregnant, we were also newlyweds and the dynamic of all these factors began to put a strain on our relationship. My wife expressed to me that she needed help and wanted me to find work in

Atlanta, but I was a bit apprehensive as things were good in Mississippi.

Our daughter is born and it's not long before I make the transition to Atlanta. I remember having five interviews and I knew I would land one of the jobs. I left my job in Mississippi sure that I would receive at least one if not five job offers. As luck would have it, I didn't even get one offer. This started a year long journey of finding full time employment. I did odd jobs here and there, and eventually found some factory work that I hated. It was long hours for little pay, and I struggled to even contribute to my family dynamic. I fell into a rabbit hole of depression and sadness. I would be so hard on myself about not being able to provide for the family I created. My wife made sure we had everything we needed during this time. She was the rock and held us down while I sought work in my field. I was able to land a few more interviews, but not land the job which added to the feeling of sadness, depression and defeat. I began to question if I was in the right field and how much longer my wife would be able to keep us afloat. This went on for a year. It was one of the toughest times of my life, but my wife would try her best to not let me get down on myself.

After more rejections I began to search in other states for employment. My wife was more than supportive and thought that if I was able to get back on my feet somewhere else it would be a smooth transition back to where she and my daughter were. I began to search aggressively, and the interviews came fast. I was in and out of town each week for about three months on interviews. However, in my field the interview process is long and drawn out so three months of interviews isn't necessarily a long time. During this time, I still applied for jobs in Atlanta because I knew how important it was to be with my wife and newborn child. I began to hear back from jobs in other states which boosted my confidence to know that I was able to impress employers enough to receive job offers. Each one I received I would pray and ask for guidance and clarity. In my heart I knew that I didn't want to be away from my family, but my head always told me I needed to provide for them by any means necessary. I was offered three jobs in three different states: Indiana, Oklahoma, and New York. I declined all three after days of prayer. It was by far one of the hardest decisions I had made to date, but I couldn't wrap my mind around leaving. I continued to apply for jobs in Atlanta and was able to make some connections and meet people who assisted me in my search. This became vital as more jobs in my field began to open.

I was finally able to land a job at Georgia State University, but as a temporary employee, only after being rejected for the initial job I applied for. Little did I know this would be the break I needed. I was able to work as a temp for about three months when two full time opportunities became available. One was the position I was currently in and the second was a job I previously applied for but did not receive an interview for. I prayed and talked with my wife about applying for the second job knowing that I was not even considered the first time the position was open. My wife provided the encouragement I needed to apply for this position and not only was I able to land an interview, but I was offered the position. I knew at that point that everything I had gone through prepared me to have a job in my field and be with my family. During this process, I would often speak with my mother and she would urge me to be patient, trust God, and His process. I did just that and was able to understand that providing for my family was not solely a monetary responsibility. I was able to learn true discernment and trust my partner knowing that she stood with me in one of the toughest times of our lives. This process also taught me the power of manifestation and praying for the things that I truly needed. I needed to be with my family but I also needed to be steadfast until all things aligned that I prayed for. I am eternally thankful that I have someone who unequivocally supports me through good and bad times while pushing me to grow as a man, a husband and a father.

7

How Will I Get Through This?
Dominiquo Johnson
McKinney, TX

In loving memory of Lorrell Askew (1979-2020)

December 31, 2019 - I am attending "Watch-Night Service" as I have done many times throughout my life. This time it all felt different, I am now living in McKinney, TX (Dallas area) and my wife and I are finally closer to my children who are only 4 hours away. My in-laws are visiting us and for the first time we are celebrating the holidays as a family. These were the thoughts going through my head as I am waiting to bring in the new year. The excitement could not be any higher. I am in a new city and state, in a new senior level management role with one of the top Fortune 500 companies in the world. At that moment, as I prepared to give my offering, I prayed to God to allow this new year to bring, growth both in my professional career and with our family, prosperity, and new opportunities.

January 6, 2020- First week of the new year and I'm expecting this year to be one of the best, if not the best years of my life. As I dropped my in-laws off at the airport, I headed to work where I was expecting to go through my first site inspection with my Regional Manager. This manager was my "acting" regional manager and other then email correspondence and video chats, we didn't have much of a rapport. Upon his arrival I introduced myself to him and directed him to an office where he could work out of.

An hour or so passed and I was asked to join him in that office. As I entered the office, our Human Resource Manager was waiting inside as well. This was odd but this company did so many other odd things, I didn't think twice about it. So, as we began the meeting, my manager's opening statements were, "Before we cover the inspections there are some things I want to address with you." My manager wanted to address the lack of hours I was spending in the office even though I was a salaried employee and would work a wide range of hours in and out of the office. I was confused and taken aback to say the least when I heard this comment.

The manager had a record of my badge scans into my office to track when I entered and exited the building. He was concerned that I was spending 35-38 hours a week in my office and not at least 50 hours. To help you get a better understanding of my role and responsibilities, I was the Security Subject Matter Expert. For this particular site, I managed all security operations, crisis management, case management, and loss and gain financial budget, alone. This role would generally provide me with a supporting staff of 2-4 personnel, but that was not the case. I was on call 24/7 to respond to any and all incidents that occurred on site. There were times when I was receiving calls throughout the middle of the night and expected to be in the office immediately with the potential of working 10 hours or more. This was a never-ending cycle. I mention to my manager the countless hours that I worked from home, only to be met by his response of, "those hours don't count." As my manager presented various scenarios insinuating that I had broken company policy, I couldn't help but to wonder why this was the first time these items were being address, particularly in this manner.

During this conversation, I found myself on a rollercoaster ride of emotions. Then at the peak of my rage emotion, I asked God to give me strength. There was an immediate sense of calm that covered my body. I then found myself not arguing or trying to defend my actions. Most people may have viewed this as a sign of defeat, but I didn't. I maintained a professional demeanor and pushed through what appeared to be an interrogation. The last words I was told was that I would be placed on paid suspension, and due to my position in the company the decision on what would happen next would have to be made from higher authority. As I gathered my things and exited the building, I knew that would be the last time I would ever return and possibly work for that company.

At that point I had spent the past two years working and moving my family to California, Virginia and then Texas. So many thoughts were going through my mind, but I knew I had to call my wife. After I explained what happened, she was just as shocked as I was, because she knew, how much time I had invested, how much I had overcome to get to where I was, and how much our family had sacrificed. She told me we would get through it, to which I responded, "I know." There was still a sense of calmness over my spirit.

Later that same day, my wife received a phone call from her mother stating that her second to oldest brother, Lorrell, was found unconscious from suffering another stroke. Her brother had a stroke a few years prior which caused physical complications, rendering his ability to walk without the aid of a cane. This time was different, he was now fighting for his life.

January 7, 2020- I received the call confirming that I will be released from my job. That following week I found out that my GPA dropped below the 3.0 requirement for my MBA course, that I was being placed on academic probation, and that I would not be able to continue my degree. I was advised by my children's mother that she would be deploying with her military unit in June and the kids would have to spend the fall in school with me; and move from San Antonio, Texas to Dallas, Texas. I am now thinking how could things get any worse and better yet how I was going to get through this!

Despite all that happened, my wife was scheduled to go back to her home office for a week in the Washington, D.C. area. My wife was going back for training as well as attending their holiday party. We both were having mixed feelings and emotions about the recent events happening in our lives, but my wife recommended that I come join her for the party and to clear my head. I, on the other hand, felt that I need to be alone, apply for jobs, and think about how I was going to fix this.

Honestly, part of me wanted to blame God. Why did he bring me here to Texas? Why now, am I facing unemployment? With all these thoughts running through my mind, I decided I needed to not be alone, so I booked a flight to D.C. and joined my wife. That weekend was fun and much needed. I would be lying if I didn't say the loss of my job impacted my mental and physical presence. There was a moment where I even got upset with my wife for trying to help me network for a potential job opportunity. The devil is so busy and knows how and when to attack you in your darkest hour. When you are all out of luck, nothing but faith in God has the ability to restore you. This was the first time I truly faced my faith in God.

During the month of February, I spent each day applying for jobs, as well as doing LinkedIn courses and training to make myself a better candidate. Given my previous role, experience, and education, I focused on six figure salaries to pick up right where I left off. I expected to wait a month maybe two before I would be back in a role with another Fortune 500 company.

March was here now and I was feeling positive about how things were going. Then the news started to break about COVID-19. My life took the most unexpected turn as this moment in life impacted the rest of the world as well. As more stories and cases of COVID-19 swept through the world, the need for interviewing and hiring went from normal to nonexistent. I was now watching the world fall apart. Everything around me was closing in fear of this virus. I was now broken and my mind filled up quickly with doubt. I knew that I still had to lead my family, be a husband, and father. The only way I would be able to do this was connecting with God, praying constantly, and keeping my faith strong.

I began waking up at 5AM to pray, read devotionals, and connect to God. This desire for connection was more than seeking answers for what I was experiencing in my life. I was seeking for more to be brought out of my own life. When I began to put God in front of my problems, God began to speak to me through everything. Since my divorce with my children's mother in 2013, my time with my kids had been primarily limited to the summer. Now with COVID-19 in effect, I was able to spend spring break with them, something I hadn't done in years. This was also the first time that I wasn't working where I had little to no time to actually spend with them.

March is also my birth month and this was the first time that I was able to share that with my children and my wife. God was answering my prayers, and I didn't realize it then.

I was now facing the months of May and June, still unemployed, which was not in my plans, nor was this something I was expecting. The biggest change during this time was my faith in God's ability to deliver. During these hard months, my marriage was severely tested. The stress of having my wife being the only one working placed added levels of stress on our marriage. I am sure my wife may have questioned if I was applying myself enough to obtain a new job, and I wouldn't fault her if she was having those thoughts, but my approach to the types of jobs I was applying for changed drastically from a six figure income to anyone who would hire me. I went from my high horse to being humbled.

Despite the all the declined emails, I didn't stop my routine of praying and connecting to God. My faith had grown to a place it had never been. I went from asking God "How am I going to get through this?" to "God *is* bringing me through this."

Through these six months of unemployment God provided me with so many blessings that I was not able to see until I was willing to give myself to him and put in the work to connect and grow as a Christian. I started off being released from a job which I thought was the best company for me to build my career. I lost my chance to continue my education for my MBA specializing in Project Management which was aligned with my career. My wife and her family were turned upside down as they waited for her brother to battle the fight of his life. Add a blended family starting a new school year for the first time in the mix, with our world facing a pandemic that had forced our nation to do almost everything virtually as the cherry on top. This was all God's plan believe it or not.

Losing my job and being removed from my MBA program gave me a chance to truly discover who I am, and who I want to be. I thought about how I was chasing the best degree that would benefit my situation the most, instead of what I felt passionate about, or really saw a career in. Not willing to give up on my desire to continue my education, I called, prayed and researched schools that would give me an opportunity. I came across Purdue University, prayed before applying, and God answered. I had time to think about how I wanted to leave an imprint on my community and beyond. The answer was through Psychology. I enrolled in their Master's in Psychology program in March and I have maintained a 4.0 GPA since being enrolled. After completion of this program I will purse my PhD in Clinical Psychology. God will get me through that as well.

In the month of July I was still unemployed, but my faith was stronger than ever. My wife and I have renovated our marriage due to the amount of time we have been able to spend together since COVID has impacted the world. I am now being a better father than I have ever been. Lastly, I have connected with God in ways I couldn't explain. I am leading a weekly Men's Ministry online with our church, I joined a forty-day prayer challenge with some close friends, and my wife and I are reading books on how we can improve our marriage. I have so much to be thankful of, God is still good.

When I stopped worrying about how long I was unemployed, I received a phone call. Just 24 hours prior, I applied to a job posting which I thought was for a driver position, but badly mistaken. I was asked to come in for an interview. During my interview I was told this role was to manage the security, safety and transportation department and all the personnel within those departments. This role was for an organization which helps at-risk youth and gives them a second and even last chance for some to get their lives on the right track. I couldn't have planned this better if I tried, but God did.

COVID-19 created unforeseen challenges and hardships. My wife and her family were faced with a hardship as her brother was placed on life-support immediately following his stroke. The doctors told them to start making plans for his passing as they couldn't see him making it through the week; that was on January 10. As I am writing this testimony, I am here to say her brother is off life support and breathing on his own. He has not fully recovered, but he is still here, only by the grace of God can I say that. Although his family cannot see him or touch him due to COVID-19, they are not mourning him. My wife's brother struggled with his own challenges in life just like the rest of us. God knew what was coming with this virus and was able to place him in a controlled environment. Even with the chaos that is ongoing in the world his family knew he was in a place where he was being taken care. God created a peace of mind for them in the middle of a pandemic.

In the midst everything else going on, the Black Lives Matter Movement was sweeping the world. I entered into a degree program prior to this movement with the hopes of helping black men, boys, women, girls and all other people of color, facing mental health issues, substance abuse issues, abuse, and the list goes on. Our communities need more professionals that look like them, to serve them. I have spent all of my life serving people. I was fighting that by chasing a dream that God hadn't designed for me.

God removed me from a situation which was destroying my marriage, fatherhood, passion, and faith. He waited until I was broken and he built me up stronger than I ever was. I spent seven months unemployed, and during that time we never missed a bill or meal. I found out more about who and what God wanted out of me during my time in the valley. God wasn't impressed with how much money I was making. God was more concerned with the lack of time I spent with him and my family. He created a series of events which took seven months for me to rebuild that brokenness, my family and my connection with him. That, is how I got through this.

8

I Love You Dude
Timothy Johnson
Syracuse, NY

During my time at North Carolina Central University (NCCU) I had the opportunity to work in Conference and Guest Services. This was probably one of the most fulfilling jobs I'd ever had but also I struggled with what my life would be without this job, and what I was going to do after college. I had one of the greatest supervisors I've ever known. The way he showed compassion, challenged me to think bigger, and the way he carried himself made me realize that the field of Student Affairs was the place for me. Throughout this testimony you'll see a variety of people that I admire, adore and/or look up to, who've given me the space to realize the I, Tim Johnson, was enough, and as long as I loved me and what I was doing nothing else mattered.

It's August 2013 and I was sitting with one of my favorite advisors, Whitney Watkins, when she says, "Alright, what are we going do about grad school plans after this summer ends and you finish this last semester?" I said "Well Whitney, I've got 12 schools on my list, I have scheduled the GRE, and I have all my recommendations solidified. However, there is one major issue. These application fees are ridiculous and I honestly do not have the means to pay for them so what should I do?" That was my biggest fear as finances seemed to be a constant in my life, making me believe that if I didn't have the means then it wasn't meant for me. Nevertheless, she looked at me and said, "You're working, so instead of buying shoes, it's time to pay application fees and get you into somebody's program that's going to pay for you to be there."

Fast forward about three months. It was now November, all of my applications were complete, I was studying for the GRE, and it was time to go home for Thanksgiving. The day before I left, I went to go see Whitney, to which she reminded me, "Make sure you submit the application the day after Thanksgiving because it's due that Friday." I look back and reply, "For sure, I got you and I will call you when I do it so that I can get the stress off of my body."

I would now like to introduce you all to another great advisor that I went to see before heading out for break, Jeremy Faulk. He too asked, "Hey buddy, how are you? Are those applications ready for submission because grad school is the only option here!" In typical fashion I look back and say "Yes Faulk, I'm going apply to grad school, don't worry I got it!"

It's now the day after Thanksgiving and I'm sitting on my parents couch with two laptops up, my phone, and a tablet. My dad had just given me the rest of the money that I needed for applications and all I had to do was push submit. Mind you, I was applying to top tier higher education graduate programs that any student would want to attend. I watched the time pass; 1p.m., 3 p.m., 3:45 p.m., 4 p.m., 4:15 p.m., 5:30 p.m., 7:10 p.m., 7:45 p.m. I closed all my devices, walked to the bathroom, and balled my eyes out. If you're thinking what I think you're thinking, then you're right, no. I did not apply for any of the graduate programs. In that moment I didn't feel competitive enough, or even smart enough to go to any of those institutions. So instead of embarrassing myself by applying I decided to cop out because I didn't think I was worth the admission. I called Whitney and said, "I am so sorry that I wasted your time, your love, and your energy towards me, I did not apply to grad school." Her next words were, "Timmy, you have let me down In a way that I cannot put into words and I just need some time as someone who loves you and appreciates you. I just need some time."

I'm back at school from Thanksgiving Break, and it's my final semester. I'm getting ready to graduate and I lose both of my on campus jobs because my supervisor transitioned out and the decision was made to cut my role. Additionally, my internship was done so I had no source of income. I got a job through the YMCA working as an ice rink operator and the best part of the job was that I got to drive a Zamboni. Four days before graduation I get a notice and I'm about to be evicted from my apartment because myself and both of my roommates had not paid rent for the last month. My folks were coming to graduation, so the amount of embarrassment I felt was through the roof. When you talk about being in a very low, dark, unworthy, unloved space, this is where Tim Johnson was paying all of his money, rent, time, and thoughts.

Graduation finally comes and as I walked across the stage to get my degree, it was actually of the five worst days of my life. Yes, family was excited, and my girlfriend at the time was happy, but for the rest of that week, I packed up my entire apartment only to move back to my parents house in Charlotte, NC where I would now share a room with my room 14 year old brother. While at home, I remember my mom coming into my room and encouraging me not to get a job, not to think about work but to just take some time to figure out what was next for me. If you know anything about Tim Johnson, me not working is a joke, so what did I do? Instead, I get not one job, but I got two, and my main job was where my mom worked which was back at the YMCA at an after school development program.

Fast forward a couple of months and it's now February. I bounced back, paid off some debt, and haven't really given grad school a lot of thought. Honestly, life seems to be OK. I had a little money in my pocket and for the first time I found some value in my life. One day during the after school program I was walking the kids up to the gym to play dodgeball and there was this little kid that I would play with all the time named Jahari. He was about 7, maybe 8 years old. He pulled me by my shirt and asked me the most life changing question one could hear in that moment. "Mr. Tim, what do you want to be when you grow up?" For the first time in my recently discovered adult life, I didn't have words to say because I was more offended that he didn't think I was already grown. When I was finally alone, I took a moment and looked around only to realize that these kids needed someone at the next level to welcome them in when they got ready to go to college, and I was supposed to be that person. Once I got home that day, I got my computer out and googled every higher education program that still had open enrollment for fall 2014.

Once I found a few programs I knew that I needed to make two very important phone calls, otherwise this next month and a half was going to be impossible. I opened my phone to call Whitney, the phone rings and rings and rings and finally she answers, "Hey Timmy, what's up!" "Whitney, I need you to forgive me for what happened last semester and help me do whatever it takes to get into a graduate program, because at this point, I will be in a grad school program come August of this year, that's it." You could hear the deep breathing going on in what felt like an eternity, as she took a moment of silence. Finally she responds and says, "Alright Timmy, but you're not going like me even after you get accepted into your program, because I'm going to be on your ass like brown on rice."

For the next month and a half I found 10 graduate programs that were still accepting applicants, applied to seven, and none of them required the GRE. I had countless interviews, applied for multiple assistantships and then played the waiting game. One day while at work, I get this email from the University of North Carolina Wilmington stating that their decision would be available in 24 hours with the provided link in the email. I was so excited, even if I was denied, it was simply the fact that I had gotten this far. I was happy that I finally took the leap.

The next day while at work the link finally became available. I opened the link and low and behold I got accepted into the program. The amount of joy that came through my heart in that moment was so astounding. All I could do was say, "Thank You, Jesus" because big homie, I wasn't sure if I was going make it. Not even 10 minutes after I look at my acceptance I get another email saying, "Hello, you've also been selected to be our new graduate assistant in the Office of Student Leadership and Engagement." If this wasn't a sign that I was exactly where I was supposed to be I don't know what is, but let me tell you something. My God does not play about me and those connected to me, and once you realize what it means to really stand on some faith and ask for help, life can dramatically change.

So, let's fast forward in time six years later, I'm still in the field of higher education. I now work at Syracuse University as the Associate Director of Student Activities and I couldn't be more excited about what is next in my life. If I had more time I would give even more testimony about the self-doubt that I carry and the imposture syndrome that goes through my mind on a daily basis, but I think it's important in this moment to focus on what got me here, which was faith and people that God used in my life to push me.

So in thinking about the title of my story "I love you, Dude," this is important to me because Jeremy Faulk and Whitney Watkins reminded me that I was loved externally, but more importantly, I needed take that and love myself internally. They taught me to transform that love into drive and passion around whatever it is that I want to be or achieve. The best feeling in the world was going back to the YMCA years later seeing Jahari and him asking, "So Mr. Tim, you still working at a college?" "Yes, I still work there." "OK bet! One day I'm going to come where you work as a college student and tell people you are reason that I am here!"

A lot of people say it's not about how you get there but when you get there. I would also add that it's not about how and when, but who and what got you there. The moment that we realize God's plan for us is designed to be the intersection for where another life can be touched and reached. All we have to do is just make to the intersection. It will never be easy and you will have a lot of days when you don't feel like you are worthy of a space, title, opportunity or even a moment, but look in the mirror and ask yourself if you don't deserve it then who does? So, take my testimony and apply these words "I love you dude, and you are worthy of everything that your heart desires."

9

Never Give Up
Jarrick Brown
San Antonio, TX

"For I know the plans I have for you, declares the Lord, plans for welfare and not for evil, to give you a future and a hope." Jeremiah 29:11.

Alpha Phi Alpha Fraternity, Inc. was important to me long before I became a member. I was first introduced to Greek life in my childhood years, and I always had the interest of becoming an Alpha or Omega Psi Phi since my dad was an Omega aspirant. Without any knowledge, I was surrounded by Alpha men; these men mentored and cared for me like I was their own son. One day I saw the letters of Alpha Phi Alpha hanging on my principal's wall. As I started conducting my research, I realized I too, had the aspirations of becoming an Alpha man. Starting with the motto, "First of All, Servant to All, We Shall Transcend All." This motto resonates with my life because I try to be successful in all my endeavors, my passion for serving others, and the belief that if you only do what is expected, you will only reach a goal of average so instead, you must reach for the stars.

Alpha Phi Alpha Fraternity, Inc., founded in 1906, is the first historically African American intercollegiate Greek-letter fraternity, making it a significant entity of Black history, especially for Black men my age.

I first applied for membership in 2013. I came well prepared for the interview with my well-polished resume from serving as the Executive Vice President of Student Government Association, former E-Board member of Campus Activities Board, Panther Advisory Leader (Freshmen mentor), chairman of the Student Committee for the 60 Million Dollar New Athletic Complex/Panther Stadium, and much more. Not to mention, my peers selected me as Freshmen and Junior of the year at our annual PV Choice Awards.

But, I didn't make it in.

At first, I was confused. I had never been turned down before. I was an A+ student, excelling in everything I did. However, that didn't change the situation. I quickly became upset. No, I was heated. I saw some of the other men who made the final cut, and I knew I was better than them. How were they able to surpass ME?

Finally, I became depressed. What was wrong with me? Wasn't I good enough? During this time, it was hard for me. As I mentioned, I went into a deep depression stage. I started listening to more and more gospel music, but if it wasn't for DeWayne Woods, I do not know how I would have made it through. He has a song named "Let Go," which eventually between one of my all-time favorite songs. The premise of the song is that when you stop worrying and allow God to have his way, that is when things start happening.

It took me months to pick myself up, but it gave me time to pray, meditate, and talk to God. It allowed me to let God back into my life. I was the student on campus who got everything he wanted from the grades to positions in various organizations. You name it and I probably got it. During this time of opening my heart and allowing God in, I was able to learn what humility was, and I can honestly say I needed to go through this to grow as a person both professionally and personally.

A year later, after I graduated from college I had the opportunity to pursue the fraternity's graduate chapter. I was finally in the process of applying for membership before my life began to take a wicked turn.

I was working two full-time jobs as the Student Manager/Retail Supervisor for Sodexo Food Services and Graduate Assistant for the Dean of the Roy G. Perry College of Engineering, all while pursuing my Master of Science in Education Administration. While visiting a doctor for a physical, he told me my blood pressure was high because of the stress I was putting on myself. So, after thoroughly considering my situation I decided to remove myself from the fraternity application process. I knew I wanted to be a member, but I knew taking the time to care for myself was more important.

"But they who wait for the LORD shall renew their strength, they shall mount up with wings like eagles; they shall run and not be weary; they walk and not faint." Isaiah 40:31. That scripture from Isaiah truly speaks on my life because if we fast forward two years to

2016, I was able to pursue the fraternity again. On November 20, 2016, at 6:05 p.m., I was initiated into the Epsilon Tau Lambda Chapter of Alpha Phi Alpha Fraternity, Inc. in Prairie View, Texas. Becoming an Alpha to me is more than wearing the letters. I have been an active worker to make sure this organization remains the absolute best as well as having worked tirelessly to help maintain the fraternity's prestigious brand.

Essentially, I want to be able to inspire others and to become a better man, and I do believe that being a member of Alpha Phi Alpha has and will continue to be cultivating in ways unbeknownst to me. I know Alpha Phi Alpha will help me leave a legacy of love and service to my fellow man.

Currently, I'm the President of my chapter serving on my second term and a secondary advisor for the collegiate chapter and it feels good. I was also able to lead my chapter in winning Chapter of the Year on both a State and Region level – making this the first time that my chapter has won this award on a regional level.

The reason I knew that it was my time in 2016 was that I prayed and talked to God about it, and knew that if I just put it in his hands that everything will be alright.

I think back to 2013 and realize how much humility I gained from being rejected. It opened my eyes to the idea that not everything you want will happen when you want it. Sometimes, you have to wait and work on yourself. Most importantly, though, just never give up.

10

November 7, 2009
Dwayne Isaacs
St. Petersburg, FL

November 7, 2009...can you remember where you were and what you were doing on this day? Take a moment to pause and think about it. For most of you reading this, it probably was just another day, but for me this is where my story begins.

When I was 27 years old, I finished my master's program and was lucky enough to land a dream job to continue to work for my alma mater. I was living in a nice new apartment, gainfully employed, had great friends, healthy and from the outside looking in, life couldn't be better. I was getting ready to go see a movie with one of my best friends. Movies were often one of my chosen ways to escape the real world so, it makes sense looking back on why on this particular day I chose to take my mind elsewhere via a movie night. Little did I know that after 27 years of bottled up emotions, secrecy, lies, and mental anguish that this would be the day that my body and mind could physically handle no more.

You see, I struggled with my sexuality for my entire life. I decided on that day, November 7, 2009, that I could no longer handle it.

My body was worn out from the lying. Bruised from the physical and mental strain of pretending. It felt like every muscle and vein were unable to continue carrying this immense burden.

It is important to know that I didn't get to this point over night. I tried everything to "fix" what I thought was broken. I read articles on how to take control of your mind. I told myself "make sure to talk about women in front of your friends", "don't say anything 'gay'", and "always talk like a straight guy...especially around your Black friends and family."

Growing up, I always knew something was different about me. I grew up in a Jamaican family and even at very young age, I couldn't understand the world I was living in. I felt my family loved me and cared about me, but at the same time, can recall buried memories of being called names and picked on for being somewhat effeminate. The music my family listened to was what I danced too, but at the same time contained messages that condemned gay people and left permanent messages in my head that all gays should die. As I write this, I can recite verbatim these lyrics of hate that are burned into my memory. I forget exactly when I made the realization that these lyrics were about people like me, but I remember the feeling of fear that was born when I did. Imagine for a moment growing up singing songs only to one day realize later on in life that the very catchy tune you enjoyed is sending a message to you saying that you should be shot and killed for being gay. We also can't forget the media of the early 90s where issues of LGBTQ+ community were becoming more and more visible. Don't ask, Don't Tell, the AIDS pandemic, young teens being killed or taking their own lives. It was becoming so very clear that being gay was not an option and I needed to fix this.

I would always ask God the same questions over and over, "Why did you make me like this? Why did you do this to me? Am I being punished?" I would ask God every single day without fail to change me and make me "normal." When you do this every single day for years, the self-hatred becomes monstrous. You don't look at yourself in the mirror, you talk down to yourself, and you become the most dangerous type of abuser. The human mind is a powerful thing, and it was when my mind decided that my prayers and pleas to God were not going to be answered that I needed to take matters into my own hands.

I asked you, as the reader, to recall what you were doing on November 7, 2009 at the beginning of this chapter. For me, I wasn't just preparing to go to the movies with my best friend. I was also preparing to take my own life because after years of turmoil, there was no other option.

I knew what had to be done. No written message, no planning, just go about your day like normal until it's time. I don't remember anything about the movie or any conversation I had with my friend because all I could think about was this would be my last night. In a strange way that brought over some sort of temporary feeling of peace that night. We made our way home and David, my best friend pulled up to my apartment and I could see that he was visibly tired and I am sure he wanted to go home. Then, the feeling right before the big drop on a rollercoaster ride came over me when it was time to get out of the car and I asked David to stay with me. I said "please, don't leave me right now". I knew once I said that, there was no turning back. My temporary peace of knowing nothing else mattered anymore had put me on a path I told myself I would never, ever explore. Somehow we ended up inside my apartment and it was not long until I broke down into uncontrollable crying and releasing years of built-up trauma. I remember him not understanding what was going on at all and I just kept asking him not to leave me. The emotional release was causing my body to become numb. I shared with him that I didn't want to live anymore. Now, I have no idea why I decided to tell him, but I did. Although it wasn't my plan to tell him, looking back on it now, I can see that it was part of God's plan all along.

It took more than two hours to finally come out to him. And it was something I told myself I would never do. I came out as gay to another person. It was single handedly the most fearful thing I have ever done in my life. If I can try to capture this feeling in words…imagine your whole body feeling light and weightless, almost like floating in a pool of water. I thought to myself, "I told someone and he is still here and saying things I didn't expect to hear." I heard, "It's ok and this doesn't change anything and I am I still your friend". He didn't want me to die. He stayed with me the entire night and almost the entire next day. He lifted me up and spoke life back into my heart. The words he used that day are fuzzy, but I remember starting to believe that I could get better. My life can be better. God had always known this and it took years of reflection to realize He heard every single prayer and was working in my life in ways I didn't allow myself to see. What I didn't see was the strategic friendships He inserted in my life with people strong in faith. God guided me to them and used them to show me what unconditional love was. He steered me to college, away from my home environment where I could find space to learn about myself in a more accepting environment. He inserted the toughest of life trials so I would learn resilience because he knew I would face them continuously as a Black gay man in this world. He inserted me into the lives of others giving me the ability to guide and be a positive role model to them which I now believe was his way of telling me that I needed to live. It turns out that I was a part of his plan the entire time and November 7, 2009 is when he called me into action. I was not supposed to take my life that day; that was not my purpose. My purpose was to get to this point today and use this platform to share my testimony.

If you are struggling like I did and had the thoughts that I had, then listen up…IT DOES GET BETTER. You are meant to be in this world and you are a part of God's plan. There is nothing he cannot get you through. He hears you, he knows the pain you feel, and he knows what's on your heart and mind. When you feel you have reached your breaking point, look to Him not for the answers, but for the strength to keep living. If you are reading this and you are in that space, find me by any means necessary. I will be your strength and support because that is what God has called me to do. You, too, have a purpose and I promise you it will get better. And to my LGBTQ+ Black men, know first-hand it can feel even more difficult for you and that there are not many role models out there for our community, but I stand here today as a now completely openly gay Black man and I hope to be as a source of hope and encouragement for you. This is my testimony and there is no question that God has guided me every step of the way to be able to share it. Now, I have made a promise to share my story in any capacity with the hopes of inspiring others like me to have live in faith and know that there are no mistakes in who you are. *"For God so loved the world that he gave his one and only Son, that whoever believes in him shall not perish but have eternal life." (John 3:16)* You are as God intended and let this story be a small reminder to that very fact.

11

Resilience, My Friend

Nathaniel Stovall
St. Petersburg, FL

As I look back over my life, one-word echoes though out it all. **Resilience!** It means the capacity to recover quickly from difficulties. These difficulties molded my perspective of life and the people who entered it at an early age. My early childhood was filled with unique experiences, as I was raised by my grandmother for the most part. My younger brother, younger sister, and I would go back and forth living between my mother and grandmother until I was about seven. You could say that my life was unstable.

During that period, I witnessed the fathers of my siblings mentally and physically abuse my mother. These are the years where children soak up things like sponges. I was building the perspective of what a man was supposed to be. I would later be molested by a family member. I would say, I never felt safe as a child. It was hard, but I continued to push through.

I was seven years old when we officially stayed only with my grandmother. I would find out a couple years later the reason that we stayed with her. My mother battled an addiction to crack and was in jail. I never saw her use it, so it came as a shock to me. This was during the era of the D.A.R.E., so it was always a time of embarrassment for me. We would have discussions about drugs, but I would never mention my mother.

I was eight years old when I gave myself to God. It was a time when everything seemed stable and safe. That would not last long. I was being raised by a woman who previously was a single mother and now raising three young children by herself. On one hand, she would make sure we always went to church and would quote bible verses. On the other hand, she would verbally and physically abuse us. It was very confusing. I was being told "I love you and you're going to be a pastor one day," then being told, "You will never be anything," while also being hit with anything that she could pick up.

During this time, my faith was being built. I was strong in my belief in God, and that was the only thing that kept me from giving up and taking my own life. I battled depression and there were many times that I wanted to end it all. I resented my mother for this. When we needed her the most, she was not there for us.

This cycle would continue until about the age of thirteen. This is the year when my mother was out of jail, going through sobriety, and living with my stepfather. It was the first time I had a role model. Things were getting a little better, but we were still living with our grandmother. The verbal and physical abuse continued. However, my faith was still strong, and I truly believed the ill treatment of me and my siblings would eventually end, which it did, at the age of sixteen or seventeen years old.

I remember that day so vividly. My grandmother and I got into a disagreement. She thought I was backtalking and swung to hit me in my face, but I grabbed her tightly and told her she would never do that again. I felt bad but I was tired of the abuse. She never laid a hand on me again. That was the same day I moved with my mother and stepfather. Later, my siblings would move out as well. I went from a dictatorship like environment into being free and not being restricted. It was the first time I was able to have friends over and go about like I pleased. It seemed like everything was going well for the first time in my life.

As I continued to take in this freedom, I would distance myself from church and God more and more. I still had the desire to go to college, but I wanted to take a year off from school. During this year I would party and drink. That was my weekly routine. I was living with no direction and care. I would drink and drive, but God continued to keep me safe. Fast-forward, to my first semester of college. I brought those past routines with me. I was struggling with completing my assignments, not due to difficulty, but the lack of focus. This forced me to fail and drop courses. I would continue this same cycle for another semester.

As I started my third semester, I experienced a major crisis. My brother was in and out of trouble with the law. My parents were constantly paying for lawyers to keep him out of jail. My mother was stressed out. At this time, my mother ended her sobriety of ten years as she and my stepfather started to use crack again.

The small business they grew began to crumble right in front of our eyes. We lost everything. We no longer had a home to call our own. I was officially homeless. I had built great relationships with a group of guys that I still call my brothers today. When I had nowhere else to go, they allowed me to live on their couch. I remember barely having enough money to purchase a couple of seventy-nine cent tacos from Taco Bell, and because I decided to be irresponsible and quit my job right before everything happened, I was also unemployed.

I had become dependent on money handouts and being able to work side jobs with my stepfather in his small business. I was really struggling inside with myself. I decided subconsciously to drown my depression with smoking, pill popping, drinking, and sex. I looked fine on the outside, but I really was not. With everything going on, I was stunned how God never left me. I stayed with my brothers for a year and a half, before I was able to move in with my aunt. This is when God was starting to reconstruct my life and take me out of depression. I was in a more stable environment and I started to get back on my feet. I decided years before that I wanted to join the Army. At that point, I was able to take care of roadblocks from past mistakes which were preventing me from joining earlier.

In 2011, I joined the Army and had my first child. I was happy to be a father. I would begin my path of finally getting my life together and experience stability. I was feeling a sense of purpose. I spent the first two years overseas in South Korea. It was hard being that far away from my son, but I continued to push through. Drinking was my vice. Drinking habits were continued to be enabled and I continued to self destruct and make irrational decisions. God was starting to call me back to him, convicting my heart to start going back to church.

In February of 2015, with my now wife, I began to go back to church. During a depressive period, one week prior to my church attendance, those irrational decisions caught up with me. I decided to go to nearby bar and have drinks. Afterwards, I drove back to the military base and was stopped at the gate per usual. When the guard smelled liquor, he immediately asked me to do a sobriety test. At that moment I knew my career was over and all I worked for was for nothing. To no surprise, I was discharged out of the Army a few months later.

This is where I know God was working for my good. During this whole transition, I was introduced to my now wife by one my good friends. She was going through her spiritual rebirth the following year and half. We started to date and I began to go to church consistently. I was changing spiritually. She was sent by God to help keep me accountable, which I have never had before. I decided to recommit my life back to Christ. Two years later, in front of our closest friends and family, we committed to spend the rest of our lives together. We moved from North Carolina to Florida and were far away from both our families.

Then, a few months after marriage we found out we were having a beautiful baby girl. You can say things were changing fast during a short period of time. There were habits that continued to pop up and cause issues. Some of these issues consisted of mismanagement of finances, binge drinking, trust, lack of how to be intimate with each other, and life perspectives. Finally, after being on the verge of our marriage flying off the cliff, I quit drinking and decided to work on my mental health and management of my money. I can say we are at a better place now. We are still growing. I always look back over my life and see how God has continued to be with me and given me a spirit of resiliency.

Resiliency, one of my closest friends, has also been present and has helped repair the relationship with my mom. She is six years sober, and saved. She is a phenomenal grandmother to my kids, and an even better mom to me. God continues to show up and remind me that a relationship with him is key in my ability to adapt well in the face of adversity.

No matter what I went through I was able to make it to the other side with God by my side. I grew from every situation. Wholeness does not happen in one day, but over time. Remember God is with you, always. As you have read over these words, I pray and hope that it encourages you to push through no matter how the situation   looks.

12

Faith and His Faithfulness
David J. Duck
Newport News, VA

Some people have fond (or not so fond memories) of being a child and going to church. They are able to recall funny incidents where "Sister So and So" forgot the words to her solo and ended up singing some Michael Jackson lyrics, or when "Deacon Whatshisname" used to shuffle around the church like Prince when he danced. I, on the other hand, had none of that. Childhood was different for me. I didn't grow up in church. I remember a brief period where my parents studied the bible with a few Jehovah's Witnesses, and I can vaguely remember a couple visits to the Kingdom Hall when I was around four or five, but I actually didn't really get formally introduced to Jesus until I was a second year in college.

Through my love for music, I joined the Black Voices Gospel Choir at the University of Virginia, and I became more and more interested in the Man we sang about. To connect deeper with the music, I had to find context for the scriptures that were in the lyrics. At least that's what I thought I was doing. I later realized that God was strategically speaking to me to connect deeper with him. He gave me several gifts (visual art, singing, playing instruments), so it was very fitting that as soon as I finally decided to use one of them to "minister" to people through song, He would began to place it on my heart to seek relationship with Him.

I've always noticed that it takes A LOT for me to worry. I've always had an internal attitude that everything would work out. Some people would call it carelessness, disengagement, or not recognizing the severity of things. I've just always felt like when things are out of your control, whatever the outcome is, is inevitable. Once I realized who was in control, that internal attitude transformed into what Christians would call FAITH. I had never been a worrier, but now I know that I don't have to worry (Psalm 46:10 Be still, and know that I am God. I will be exalted among the nations, I will be exalted in the earth!), because God holds the world in His hands. So, in the early stages of my walk with God, through graduation from undergraduate school, graduation to graduate school, several jobs, joining my first church, marrying the love of my life, and having our first child, I saw that He never failed me. His Word is true. He never left me or forsook me. He showed up and showed out in EVERY situation. It was almost like because He knew I trusted Him so much, that He wanted to honor my faith by coming through. EVERY. TIME. This caused my faith to become the strongest aspect of what made me a follower of Christ. Eventually, I knew there may come a time where my faith would be tested---I just didn't know when, but I was confident that when it came, it wouldn't make me waiver because I KNEW that God is able. But, as life goes, I ended up running into a situation that made me question my faith, and question God.

At the end of 2015 my wife and I had our first child---a beautiful baby girl. The pregnancy, labor and delivery had minimal complications, and outside of a common slightly-elevated bilirubin level, everything seemed perfect. And it was. If it wasn't for my daughter being born so close to Christmas, we actually would have discharged from the hospital in half the time. At the time, my wife and I had only really decided that we wanted one child. Having another one was a road we would cross if it came up, but it was not in our immediate plans. As our daughter started growing into a smart, outgoing, little lady who is full of personality, and after giving her everything she wanted, we decided that our family would feel even more complete if God blessed us with a son. So, naturally, when 2018 rolled around and we found out my wife was pregnant again, we prayed that God would round our little family out by allowing us to birth a boy. We were completely content with the fact that whatever God blessed us with was meant to be, but I asked God for a son, and because of my faith, I knew He would do it. Therefore, it wasn't a surprise to me when we went the 20 week appointment, and the nurse did the ultrasound and typed "I'M A BOY" on the screen. It was just God showing me that we would "give us the desires of our heart" (Psalms 37:4 "Delight thyself also in the LORD; and he shall give thee the desires of thine heart"). My wife (Tiffany) and I were excited and felt like our little family was now even more complete.

This pregnancy came with a bit more discomfort than the first. More nausea and pain, but we chalked it up to her carrying a male child, and that somehow being vastly different than when she carried our daughter. Additionally, with our first child, Tiffany was induced on the due date because there was no sign of labor coming, but this time, we were awakened in the middle of the night by contractions. Rushing to the hospital (which was about 70 miles away…that's an entirely different story) at 5 a.m. with contractions every four minutes was a challenge in itself, but by the grace of God, we made it safely for Tiffany be admitted. We were met with several different challenges during her roughly 14 hours of labor. We almost missed the epidural window because the anesthesiologist was backed up, then when he showed up, he had to stick her several times to get it right. Then, in the early evening, our baby boy was born! We breathed a sigh of relief, and thanked God for His magnificent blessing.

Over the course of the next 24 hours, everything seemed normal. Baby Nathan latched on to mom like a pro, family made the 70 mile trip to visit, and my mother even brought our daughter with her to meet her little brother. We were finally starting to see the light at the end of this tunnel. Now the only thing left to do was to get discharged. One of the items on the discharge checklist is to ensure the baby had created a wet diaper. Nathan, apparently had not wet his diaper yet. The nurses said that typically, a wet diaper should appear within the first 24 hours, and if it didn't happen in the first 36 hours, it would be a cause for concern. He was drinking breastmilk fine, and seemed completely ok. But I felt in my spirit that something wasn't right.

36 hours passed by, with me checking what seemed to be every 5 minutes to see if the yellow line on the front of his diaper had turned blue yet. STILL NOTHING. Tiffany was still recovering, so I

didn't want to worry her, as labor was rough, but I was starting to become very unsettled. When the nurse came in to check, she seemed perplexed that he still had not wet the diaper. She tried some rudimentary tricks to get him to go (adding slight pressure to his bladder, running warm water), but nothing worked. At this point, they decided to bring in a pediatrician to take a look. The pediatrician said everything looked normal, so he would have to take Nathan downstairs to try to insert a catheter and do an EKG to see if his bladder actually contained any urine. At this point, we were very nervous, and I began to pray. "God, please allow everything to be ok. Allow the catheter to empty his bladder and let us go home!"

When the pediatrician came back, he had a look on face that made my heart sink. He stated that he saw some urine in the EKG, but could not get any to come out in the catheter. We knew for sure something was wrong with our baby. He said the only thing he could do was to call in one of the ONLY two pediatric urologists in the state, to assess what was going on. They took Nathan to the Neonatal Intensive Care Unit (NICU), started to supplement him with formula (thinking maybe he wasn't getting enough milk from the breastfeeding), and then the Urologist took a look at him. We waited. We prayed. Waited. Prayed. After what seemed like forever, the Urologist comes back into the room, and has the same look the Pediatrician had earlier. He told us that he believed our son had something called posterior urethral valves---flaps of extra skin near the opening of the bladder that prevent urine from exiting. The issue is, as the bladder fills up and urine can't exit, the urine will travel back into the kidneys (if it hadn't already) and that can cause serious complications (ultimately, kidney failure....which means transplant....or at his age...death). He also mentioned that the walls of his bladder seemed thicker than normal. Tears started to well up in our eyes. Why would God allow this?

The pediatric urologist went on to say that there is a procedure that could be done that involved taking an instrument through the opening of the urethra and removing the flap of skin. We saw a glimmer of hope! The catch was he would not likely be big enough to survive that procedure until he was at least two years old. That meant that in order for Nathan to eliminate urine properly until he could get the procedure, he would have to spend the first two years of his life with his bladder literally stapled to the outside of this pelvis, and allowed to empty straight into his diaper. He would have no chance of a normal life that a healthy little boy would have. He would have to be very careful with how he moved and we would have to be very sensitive to the fact that he has a major organ on the outside of his body. We were crushed. The urologist said he still had not confirmed that he indeed had posterior urethral valves, but he would have to do a particular test to find out. That was on Monday afternoon. He would not be able to perform the test until Friday or the following Friday. So we were stuck in the hospital for the whole week with our precious, innocent little boy downstairs in the NICU, where we could only see him periodically.

During this time, MANY things were going through my mind. I was devastated, but I had to attempt to be strong for Tiffany. The truth was, many times, I felt like she seemed stronger than me. She had gotten into a solid routine of going down every three hours to nurse him and spend time with him---making sure he knew that we were still there. Her strength gave me strength. Sometimes, while she rested, I would go visit Nathan in the NICU to pray over him. There I would see other babies that were battling for their life, and parents that have been doing these visits for months. On the one hand, it saddened me to think about what this could turn into. On the other hand, I felt convicted for not having that faith that I was so accustomed to---for worrying about this situation when God has come through for me EVERY. TIME. I also felt convicted because in comparison, our situation felt way less severe than some of the other families'. Even still, sometimes, while Tiffany was feeding, I would have to go get in the car, and take a quick ride to let my emotions out. I would pull over and CRY. CRY out to God to heal my son. Cry out to God to soothe my wife. Cry out to God to give me strength. In those moments, I would feel better, but there was still a cloud over me that I couldn't shake---and God knew that.

While visiting Nathan one time, the NICU nurse informed us that she was able to use a smaller catheter and successfully remove a large amount of urine! This was the first sign that our miracle was on the way! We were not in the clear yet, because while they were able to get urine out, that did not rule out the potential valve condition. We were just relieved that kidney damage was looking less likely, but the Friday test was still looming. At any rate, I knew God was giving me a sign that HE WAS STILL GOD, and he could do the unthinkable, the unimaginable, the impossible. That gave the spark I needed to carry on, and put my faith to work! I began to try to operate like the miracle was already done, and started to try to bring some normalcy to my family's life as much as I could.

While Nathan was in the NICU, my wife actually had to be discharged. At that point, she was no longer the patient, Nathan was. So we had to figure out somewhere to stay. The thought of having to stay in a hotel nearby, with Tiffany needing to go see Nathan to feed him every three hours seemed hectic and daunting. That's when we saw God's hand moving again. One of the nurses knew what we were dealing with, and allowed us to stay in the mother/infant unit room after being discharged! As long as the unit did not fill, we were able to stay there, free of charge, while we awaited his test. While staying there, I decided what we needed to help bring us some brightness was to see our daughter. So, I drove the 70 miles home to pick her up from daycare, and brought her back up to the hospital to stay with us for a couple of days. Seeing the care-free innocence of that little girl helped me to worry less, and trust that God was in control. We ventured out one day to the library, to grab food, and try to regain that normalcy, while we waited to watch God work a miracle. My faith was growing stronger every moment. During one of my prayers, I cried out to God and said "God. I can feel you working. Make it plain to me! Show me the miracle. Remove the blockage in the MIGHTY NAME OF JESUS!"

During one of my visits to the NICU, I noticed something in Nathan's catheter tubing. Small little solids (chunky piece of *something*), were seemingly marching out away from him in his urine. That was when I knew I was witnessing a miracle!!!!!! I literally saw the blockage being removed. Listen. It wasn't a nurse reporting it to me. I saw it with my own eyes. 15 to 20 little chunks floating in his urine. I asked the nurse what it was. She tried to explain it as sediment that may have been sitting there because of how long the urine sat in his bladder, but something told me…THIS was the issue. Sediment or valves, God was removing them, and He wanted me to see it. I ran up to the room to tell my wife. God was doing it! We gave Him glory, and kept our focus to see this situation to the end.

The nurse said because Nathan had been producing so much urine, that she was going to remove the catheter, and see if he would go on his own. If he could, it was a very low chance that he had the valves the urologist suspected. Again, by the grace of GOD, in no time, she removed it, and my boy soaked that diaper!! He continued to urinate normally, and we felt a huge sigh of relief. Our miracle was here. We could feel it. The only thing left to do was to get the urologist to confirm what we knew God had done. Later that Wednesday, we got a call that the urologist was so pleased with the reports he had been receiving, that he would come and run the test for the valves early. As soon as he completed the test and we could get Nathan circumcised, he could be discharged. The next morning, we visited the NICU and Nathan wasn't there. The nurse said he was on his way back, and that the test was SUCCESSFUL. There was NO SIGN OF POSTERIOR URETHRAL VALVES, and the urologist was signing off on his discharge! We were SO EXCITED! The only instruction was that we had to go see another urologist in one week to get another EKG to ensure everything was ok.

We took Nathan home, and like they asked, we took him to the other pediatric urologist in the state, and he confirmed that our son was PERFECTLY HEALTHY. Not only had God fixed the issue, he made it so that it looked like it never existed. I drove back from that appointment in pure awe of the power of our Lord. I want everyone who reads this to know that God is a healer! Big or small--- God can truly do exceedingly, abundantly above ALL that we can ask or think! You may feel your faith waiver, but if you ask Him for peace, and stay focused, He will reveal His glory. As I type this, Nathan is now exactly 14 months old, and I can't seem to keep enough diapers in the house to keep up with how much he uses them---and I wouldn't trade that for the world.

Isaiah 41:10 "So do not fear, for I am with you; do not be dismayed, for I am your God. I will strengthen you and help you; I will uphold you with my righteous right hand."

13

Sunday Mornings
Joshua Wilson
Tampa, FL

Growing up, I have vivid memories of Sundays. Sunday mornings were always the same, in that at around 7 a.m. My mother would yell for my sister and me to get ready. My mother always had the goal for us to be on time for church, though we rarely made it on time. The car was tuned and primed with the gospel, and the worship started before we walked in the church doors. We often rolled into the early morning service in time for a couple of songs, benediction, offering, and Sunday School. Sunday church was highly valued for our family growing up in Birmingham, Alabama. My parents divorced when I was six-years-old, and we moved around a lot. No matter how far away we lived, we made it to church on Sundays. It was there where I would know to love the Lord and would give myself to Christ. It's where I learned of Christ's values and made a commitment to walk in those values.

I spent 21 years at this old Birmingham church before I left Birmingham for Muncie, Indiana. It was there where I fully recognized what I had yet to understand, that I had grown stagnant in my faith. It had become more of a ritual than a purposeful driven experience.

In high school, I never saw myself leaving Alabama. It wasn't until college and my interest in graduate education that would lead me from home. My mother believed in education. She encouraged my sister and me to attain a college degree, as early as grade school. Despite my awful high school grades, she had already laid out the path that I would be heading to college. She had big dreams for us and would do anything to help us succeed. Mom was very encouraging of graduate school education, and I knew she was proud. Upon my arrival at graduate school in small-town Muncie, I learned quickly of a Baptist church that many of my Black peers recommended. That first service, I'll never forget being somewhat nervous but excited. It was a natural fit, but more importantly, I found a new spark. The worship was energizing, and I was learning again through the sermons. Every week I was able to recall what we learned. It didn't feel like a show. It was the word, and the word was good. The church has been my rock through my life, and I have experienced too many blessings to name. Yet my faith has been tested in this journey with Christ.

Working in higher education, the pay is not great. Entry-level professionals often make less than teachers with a master's degree. Living 12 hours away was also financially difficult. Looking back, I don't even know how I made the financial situation work to make it home for Thanksgiving and Christmas. There were some times when I had to use Coinstar to turn those coins into cash around the holidays. My third year of living away from home was a rough time for the family.

December 2011, my mother would have a stroke forever rocking her world. Just two months after the stroke, while at home recovering by herself, her house was struck by a tornado. My prayers were loud, and I was scared. What was God trying to communicate to me through these circumstances? When the tornado struck so close after the holidays, I didn't have enough money to go home to support her in that time. Fortunately, lots of family members were there to support her. Already contemplating if it was time to move closer to home, I now had a definitive answer even if it was "traditionally" too soon to make a work change for my career path.

A few months later, I would find myself in Florida, a much better driving distance than South Bend, Indiana, with better pay. God is good. Yet I still internally battled if I should have committed to return to Birmingham considering my mother's health. We learned that she needed a kidney as hers was declining in function. Fortunately, we had some time before the necessary measures to be taken. All to say, why didn't I read the signs? Why did I miss on key moments to support her? Yet, she supported me all the while. She vacationed and visited Florida, so proud of me, and the joy from her certainly brought me joy.

My world would again be rocked in 2018. We learned that her kidney had reached a red alert, in addition to learning that she had breast cancer. An outpatient surgery scheduled after Thanksgiving started a downward health trend for which memories still haunt me when I think of that time. Complications post-surgery revealed other health problems that would require additional surgeries. After making it through what seemed to be an incredible firestorm of possibilities, she was well on a recovery path. It was during this period where she unexpectedly passed in the night. I'll never forget the call from my sister. I had so many plans for my mother and me because I believed she deserved the world. She was just a cute woman waiting for me to find my wife and selfishly wanting grandchildren. She was a selfless woman who brought so much life to our family.

Sometimes I am angry at God. I pretend not to have this feeling, but it is real. It's easy to be angry at God for being God-driven and growing up in the church, yet not having a wife. It's also easy to blame God for the passing of my rock, my mother, two years ago. However, when those fleeting thoughts arrive, they battle with the notion that it is also easy to blame God and not myself. It's easy to forget that he has a plan for us all. It's easy to forget that my problems are minuscule in his presence, yet he still has a purpose for me. It's easy not to think about all of the incredible blessings he has provided me and continues to provide me daily. So then, my mind wonders with the endless what-ifs, and I encourage myself to continue to lay my burdens upon him who can handle it better than me. This is a continuous process as I'm still healing. I'm working on forgiving myself and working on trusting in Him. As hard as it is to acknowledge this pain I carry, I know that his love is greater than I can ever imagine. "For I know the plans I have for you," declares the Lord, "plans to prosper you and not to harm you, plans to give you hope and a future" Jeremiah 29:11 NIV.

14

The Architect Who Defines Your True Purpose

Brandon Ashe
Henrico, VA

The ultimate journey that we as men choose to embark on is finding ones' true purpose in life.

We tend to allow our success and accomplishments define who we are as individuals. Unfortunately, success and accomplishments don't define ones' true purpose. During this particular journey, we encounter a multitude of distractions that will try and derail what we are truly destined for. Insecurities, self and spiritual doubt, depression, and questionable decisions can begin to mount as you progress.

God's plan has and always will be the blueprint to understanding ones' true purpose. We as black men tend to be brought up in a culture that raises us in the belief that we have to be immune to emotions and that we have to be strong for ourselves and all that are in our circle. As life begins to mount on our shoulders, two thoughts are normally asked through our prayer's: "Who can I talk to?" and "I need help." Through this, God hears your cries and begins to right your ship which allows you to reset and refocus on what he has ordained for you as your true purpose.

I've gone through life with God ordering my steps and even still experience a season of darkness every now and then. God has been my architect since the beginning of time but in my early years I felt that I was in control of EVERTYHING. The one mistake I've always made is not allowing God's voice to echo through important events in my life. I always feel as if I need to be in control over every aspect. One particular event humbled me in ways that opened my eyes to how impactful my purpose was going to be.

The year was 2005, high school was coming to an end, and I finally received my acceptance letter to my college of choice. Life was good, I had all that I could ever want in life at that time, until one memorable spring morning. I was in the living room watching TV when my parents came in. I could tell that they were getting ready to talk to me about something important. They had recently returned from Chicago from an appointment for my father at the Mayo Clinic, as had been experiencing extreme fatigue for a couple months. They had received a diagnosis from his local physician a while back but wanted a second opinion which prompted the Mayo Clinic visit. I remembered the moment I locked eyes with my father and asked him what was wrong with him. "Pancreatic cancer," he replied, "I have pancreatic cancer son." The indescribable moment of numbness and disbelief covered my body as I began to feel a physical pressure like no other.

I ran from the house, jumped in my car, and began to pull off with no direction as to where I was heading. I began to ask God "Why me?" "Why my father?" and then came the tears. An uncontrollable feeling of pain and sadness came over me as I heard a knock on the window. It was my younger brother who was headed home from playing outside. I asked him to get in the car as I knew my parents hadn't told him yet. All I remember saying to him was "Dad has cancer." We sat at the stop sign for a couple minutes in silence as we tried to digest our feelings. In my own thoughts all I could think about was how could God do this to me? I wanted answers.

Fast forward to freshmen year in college, my relationship with God wasn't anywhere close to where it once was. As my father's condition and appearance began to decline so did belief in my God. No matter how hard I prayed it seemed to fall on deaf ears as my father continued to get worse. Always in good spirts and full of positivity, he did his best to keep me smiling and happy every time I came home from college. I needed that. I knew he was in a lot of pain because of the treatments, but he still kept me as his primary focus to make sure that I was keeping my head up by remaining close to God.

Almost a year to his diagnosis, God began to plant the seed of understanding of what he had in store for my father and what he was beginning to sew in me for years to come. I began understanding what my father's purpose was in my life: my teacher and my hero. The knowledge and teachings he was able to give me throughout my early years were God's blueprints of how I must continue to walk in my faith and trust in Him after my father was gone.

Tuesday, October 3, 2006 my father took his last breath on this earth. I remember being at the grave site as I watched them lower the casket into the ground. At that precise moment, it hit me: my life had forever changed and I was about to begin the journey of understanding what my true purpose was through my own eyes.

Its been 14 years since my father has passed. I'm married now with a child of my own, a far cry from the 20-year-old kid he left as he departed this earth. As I look back on everything that I've endured and accomplished over my journey thus far, I find myself wishing that he was still around to bask in all of my accomplishments and Gods' blessings with me. The death of my father sparked a new found freedom and love for the spiritual side of my life that I hated for so many years. His death taught me a couple things worth sharing.

First, you will always have a true purpose in God's plan. No matter how confusing and tough life may be, remember that each and every day you wake with God's grace, health and strength, you still have a purpose, and you still have God's plan to reveal. Second, as a man, it is ok to release and feel emotions that we've been taught to suppress. Being mindful that we are human too, its ok to feel pain, sadness, and regret just like we feel happiness, joy and blessings. Finally, above all, live by the old saying; "Let go and Let God." If you actively meet God just an inch in the right direction when it comes to making the right decisions in life, he will take you the rest of the way.

Life will never be easy, sometimes finding your true purpose gets lost or out of focus. Remember that sometimes it may be an event or a person or both, but God's plan will take you through a season of reckoning like no other that will ultimately reveal your true purpose in life.

Use God's faith and remember as my mother always tells me; "You are more than a conqueror. Greater is he in you than he that is in the world, you can do all things through God who strengthens you."

15

The REAL Superman
Brandon Artis
Charlotte, NC

Anyone who knows me is aware of my affinity for Superman. My friends can trace it back to my America Online (AOL) instant messenger days, and my fanaticism transitioned to today's social media aliases, multiple tattoos, and enough paraphernalia to have a Superman themed room in my home. It's also ignited many hours of debate over the superiority of Marvel vs. DC comics and who would win in hypothetical fights between Superman, Batman, the Hulk or whoever is top of mind. However, it was always funny to me when people reacted to my blank stares when they tried to connect over some random and obscure fact reserved for the hardcore comic book fans. "How could you choose Kal-El over Tony Stark?!" Kal who? I said I like Superman! (If you're as lost as I was the first time I heard this, "Kal-El" is Superman's birth name on his home planet, Krypton.) Needless to say, I learned a lot of classic Superman lore by accident over the years. But no one knew the true roots of my fanaticism. It was for the REAL Superman, at least in my eyes… Willie R. Artis, Sr. – my grandfather.

For as long as I can remember, my grandfather, also known as "Randolph," lived in my home. I was raised by a single mother, and she took care of her father who also served as my father figure in his later years (he was already 60 years old when I was born), but I never paid attention to his age. He was always just the fun-loving cool old man that would sneak me cookies and candy, give me money, and let me stay up late to watch his Atlanta Braves and old westerns with him. I knew of all his health issues, but the true impact wasn't registering in my young brain. I was there to see my mother preparing needles and meticulously drawing fluids out of bottles to precise levels, followed by multiple plucks of the needle to eliminate air bubbles and get a more accurate reading. Then, every day she would give him the shot of insulin in his stomach.

I also saw Randolph prick his finger, put the drop of blood on a tab and insert it into a little machine that would cause a reading to pop up on the screen. And he had this container labeled for every day of the week with all his pills in it, so he could just open the compartment for the day and take what was in there. It all looked fun to me. I wanted to take the pills and give him the shot too, but my mother obviously wouldn't let me.

It wasn't until I entered high school that I realized the extent of my grandfather's declining health. He had high blood pressure, high cholesterol, diabetes, two strokes, and three heart attacks (I'm probably missing multiple other ailments in there too.) Yet, he always seemed to bounce back! He would stay in the hospital a few days, maybe a week, and return home back to his tricks, returning to the neighborhood where he lived most of his life and running his "cat house" (as my uncle called it) where all the old heads would go to drink, smoke and gamble. While he didn't drink or smoke anymore, he owned and operated the place and it's probably what kept him going. He had a sense of purpose and people depending on him, so as soon as he was healthy enough to walk with his cane, he would be back at the house. Randolph always seemed to pull through, despite what any of the tests said. It was for all these reasons that my grandfather's doctor of over 30 years referred to him as his "miracle patient," but I just called him "Superman."

Fast forward a few years – I had just graduated with a degree in Broadcast Journalism. For those old enough to remember, that also coincided with the "Great Recession" of 2008. So, there I was, fresh out of school with no solid job prospects while trying to break into an industry where it was already notoriously tough to start a career. I decided to go back home to figure things out, and my mother welcomed her only child back with open arms. It wasn't a bad deal – I took a job at Geico as a claims agent living rent free and making more money than I ever had at that point in my professional journey. I was around family, and had the freedom and means to travel as I pleased.

Now, as someone who was used to accomplishing everything I put my mind to, this proved to be a unique period in my life. I was the type of person who set my mind to something and achieved it almost every time. That caused me to feel frustrated when people would ask me, "So, when are we going to see you on

TV?" The bad economy spiel could only last so long for someone who was such a go-getter. There was no good excuse. I always found a way to win. Being honest with myself, I realized I had become complacent. I was way too comfortable just milling about with an easy job and comfortable living situation. I had given up on my dream career. I was no longer pushing myself for more. It just so happened that this time of introspection also allowed me to be more aware of Randolph's health rapidly diminishing. He wasn't bouncing back as quickly as he used to, but he was still trucking.

Have you ever experienced a moment when it felt like you were outside of your body and watching a scene unfold? That moment for me was August 25, 2009. I was there, but it felt like I was watching a movie. I vividly remember being awaken by the nurse in our home early in the morning – "Brandon, I think you should go be with your mother. Your grandfather is transitioning." I immediately jumped up and ran in his room to see my mother sitting across from him with tears in her eyes as he lay in his bed. I could tell he was on the way out. He was motionless with just a slight trace of life left, and within mere minutes, gone. I witnessed the exact time he exhaled his last breath.

Needless to say, the next week was a blur. We already had his affairs in order. There was no confusion on next steps. But there were still lots of people in and out of the house, lots of calls, lots of cards, lots of laughs, and stories about him – some I knew and plenty I didn't. And then, it was over. All the hustle and bustle stopped, and it was just my mother and I in the house. That's when my mind got to rest and I felt distraught. Days, weeks, and months went by, and I felt like I was stuck in mud. I felt out of control like I was driving on black ice, and I knew I was just going through the motions. I was not fulfilled, nor was I living a life of abundance as God promised. Why does my cup look empty? I thought it was meant to run over! I began to doubt Him, myself, and all the goals I had lined up that slowed to a halt in recent years. Still, I prayed a lot – not for anything specific, but just for a sign of showing me where I was supposed to go. I was lost, and I just wanted some direction. "Lord, I don't know where I'm supposed to be, but I know there's something else I'm supposed to be doing."

One night, my grandfather came to me in a dream. It didn't seem like anything spectacular, but he said, "Stop worrying. Things will work out. I got you!" The next morning, I woke up with a feeling of peace over me for the first time in months. All the anxiety was gone. I still did not know what was to come, but I knew things would be fine. I think that was a tag team effort between God and my grandfather, because I got up saying, "For I know the plans I have for you, says the Lord. Plans for good, and not for disaster to give you a future and a hope!" – Jeremiah 29:11.

Needless to say, I jumped out of bed with more pep in my step than I'd had in a long time. I was energized. Motivated for the first time in a long while. I still didn't know what was to come, but I knew to just keep my eyes open and be ready to receive the blessing when it came – whatever and whenever it did. Spoiler alert: when God shows up, HE SHOWS UP BIG!

In short, I made the decision that I wanted to go back to grad school and within eight months, God had me in a position to pick between multiple schools with my tuition paid for in-full along with a grad assistantship (and later an internship) related to my field that provided me additional income. I did not have to take out one loan. What a turnaround! It was a complete 180-degree flip from feeling like I had no direction to understanding exactly what I wanted to do. Those events propelled me into my current career where I am very satisfied and on track to be a partner in my firm in just a few short years!

My cup is certainly full, especially as we are living in uncertain times. 2020 has been a year for the history books... the COVID-19 pandemic, an ambiguous election year, unemployment yet again at a record high – even as I sit here now in my home and type this from Charlotte, NC, I just experienced an earthquake that shook my house for minutes – I AM NOT SUPPOSED TO EXPERIENCE EARTHQUATES HERE!

I do not know what is to come, but what I do know is I continue to meditate on God's word. I have three Superman-themed tattoos, and while they portray me as a fanatic at first glance, they are a constant reminder of how my grandfather brought me a message from God over ten years ago to not worry. My tattoo of the entire verse of Jeremiah 29:11 on my forearm reminds me that God is always in control, and that He will shift things in my favor when the time is right. I will not be anxious or afraid. I am still expecting overflow. I know it's coming, because my back is watched by both God and the REAL Superman!

16

Watching Plants Grow

dr t leon williams
Charlotte, NC

When I was in grade school, one of the most fascinating homework assignments was growing a seed in a cup. I distinctly remember bringing my first plant home from school. Every day, I would anxiously run to the window seal hoping to see some sign of progress. For some unapparent reason, I was drawn specifically to what lies beneath the soil. After ten days, the first sign of life appeared—a leafy green stem had broken through the soil. Although I was elated to see growth, I was more curious about the growth pattern. Later in life, I would learn that this process is called germination—growth of a plant contained within a seed.

This childhood learning exercise would become a defining moment in my life. It was at this appointed time that I realized that my hunger for deeper understanding was my gateway to making meaning of life at a much greater depth. For the rest of my grade school years and throughout middle and high school, I eagerly searched for greater understanding. The older I got, the deeper the inquiry. By high school, I found myself engaged in conversations, listening but also actively thinking about what lies beneath the surface. Unintentionally, my mind would gravitate to key words and phrases, emotions, and body language but the greatest draw was the heart connection.

Conversations with family, friends, neighbors, and strangers spoke differently to my heart. Impulses, anxieties, nerves, and triggers stood in the shadow of every conversation. Words were less important, body language told half the story, and emotions were masked. I found that truth is hidden in our hearts and we often guard our hearts to avoid being transparent and vulnerable.

At one point, I asked God, "What is going on? Why is this happening? What are you trying to show me? Why are you giving me access to people's deepest thoughts and emotions?" It was not until my adult years that God revealed to me His purpose of gifting me with access to the heartbeat of His people. In other words, God allowed me to mature before entrusting me with His people. Through God's spiritual lens, I was able to share in the lived experiences of others, be it sorrow, hurt, pain, suffering, concern, confusion, panic, crisis, as well as joy, love, peace, justice, kindness, and respect.

This spiritual revelation has allowed me to walk in solidarity with others, especially, My Brothas. Now, you may be wondering how so? Well, God afforded me the opportunity to lean into the conversation with anticipation of hearing Him. More pointedly, I believe that God was speaking to me through the experiences of others. Instead of lingering in the matters of the heart of others, solidarity came in the form of mirrored experiences. This dual-purpose prohibited me from disengaging and disembodying My Brothas' lived experiences.

As I listened more intently, I heard my voice. I imagined my experiences. I felt my expressions. I observed my mannerisms. I recognized my cry. I saw wet tears on dry faces. I was drawn beyond their personal stories and concerns. Initially, I thought God had spiritually allowed me to sit in their seat of desperation but instead I was sitting in my own seat. As a result, I listened closely with a sense of urgency for the purpose of liberating My Brotha as well as myself.

Please allow me to reemphasize an earlier point, germination is the growth of a plant contained within a seed. Watching plants grow has taught me to step outside myself to see myself. To not only examine what lies beneath the surface of a man but also to turn the light inward to examine my own evolution of growth.

Since grade school, my attention and energy focused on others but now my perspective is shared. The burden of life is shared. The weight of the world is shared. Pain and suffering are not my own. This shared perspective eases the pressures of life. Now, I can decompress knowing that I am not alone. There is a sense of relief that I don't have to be strong alone.

Little did I know that God was preparing me to take a hard, in-depth look at myself. The concept of watching plants grow has not only brought me to a point of contact with My Brothas. It has also brought me to a point of knowing self. Not only that, the days of listening for God through the lived experiences of others created a pathway for listening for God through my own experiences. Now, every encounter, conversation, and engagement have new meaning.

Collectively, I learned that our experiences link undisclosed truths that fashion our reality, which further complicates navigating life. For many reasons, we have learned to suppress truth to protect our Blackness, masculinity, humanity, and pride. We have also hidden mistrust, insecurities, and inferiority further deepening systemic injustice and inequality. As a result, we speak and act from a place of discontent, anger, frustration, discomfort, and mediocrity.

We have become masters of masking our pain and feelings. We are often agitated about who we are and who we are not. In many circles, this reality can be interpreted as the storms of life. Rain, snow, heat, cold, wet, dry, all of which agitate the seed. Unlike earthly plants, these conditions regardless of the season are necessary for growth. It is to our advantage to embrace, honor, respect, dignify, and love the germination process.

Let me be perfectly clear, the storms of life are not meant to punish you. If this was so, then Jesus' journey to the cross is invalid. Hebrews 12.6 (NKJV) asserts, "For whom the Lord loves He chastens, and scourges every son whom He receives." Our experiences are meant for correction and discipline, not punishment. God loves you. God, through His grace and mercy allows or places you in experiences for correction and discipline. Why? The scripture above says that He loves you.

This perspective can only be appreciated and best understood if you turn the light inward. Watching plants grow ultimately is an inward transformation and public testament to God's mighty hand over your life. Hebrews 12:5 (NKJV) reads, "My son, do not despise the chastening of the Lord, nor be discouraged when you are rebuked by Him." In other words, do not hate, regret, or lose hope. Be unwavering in spirit. Our experiences are designed by God for steadfastness and steadfastness is being bound to your duty regardless of the storm.

Some may argue that the seed is everything. Others may say that the storms of life shape who we are. 1 Corinthians 3:7 (NLT) asserts, "It's not important who does the planting, or who does the watering. What's important is that God makes the seed grow."

I am honored to be your brother and friend. In my mind, Brotherhood is a distinct sacred connectedness with God's creation. I have no hostility towards you, My Brotha. I am at peace with you, My Brotha. I love you, My Brotha. I support you, My Brotha. I want to help you, My Brotha. I understand you, My Brotha. I want to listen to you, My Brotha. I am not afraid of you, My Brotha. I trust you, My Brotha. I need you, My Brotha. I will advocate for you, My Brotha. I have confidence in you, My Brotha. I can relate to you, My Brotha. I will defend you, My Brotha. Why? I am you.

17
Redeeming My Path
Kevin Clark
Chicago, IL

Growing up in Pittsburgh in the late 80's was hectic, and food was scarce. Now, none of that had to do with Pittsburgh or money being tight, and more to do with growing up with six siblings, four brothers and two sisters. Our home was a madhouse of kids, and I wouldn't have it any other way. If you were five minutes late to dinner, chances are you were going to bed hungry, but you learned to be on time. Elbowing each other on the couch so you didn't have to be the odd one out on the floor watching TV, taught you to be tough and have thick skin. Then there were the family vacations, nine humans packed into a van designed for seven for what seemed like endless hours upon hours of staring out the window and just wishing you could go outside and play with your friends. What did we all learn from that you ask? Before 2020 I would have said not much, but now I understand the greatest lesson my parents taught me was bestowed during the Wednesday night church kid's club we attended every week growing up.

To this day, I can still remember heading to church every Wednesday night. I would help my mom and dad setup the blue tarp in the gym, and then play around with my friends until it was time to begin. Every club night would start with a song, and one of the final songs we would sing before the lesson and game for the night would be that week's memory verse. One night still sticks out in my mind, and that's when we memorized Proverbs 3:5-6. Even as I recite it in my head after all these years, I can't help but speak it in a sing-song fashion: "Trust in the Lord with all your heart and lean not on your own understanding; in all your ways acknowledge him and he will direct your path." I didn't know it at the time, but as this earworm of a verse burrowed into my head it would go on to be one of the guiding forces in my life, as well as one of the most humbling.

All throughout middle and high school it was all I could do to share my faith with anyone who would listen. I enjoyed church and was always eager to volunteer to help on Sunday or during the week. I spent my summers traveling all over Western Pennsylvania putting on Vacation Bible Schools and had a passion for reaching kids. During high school, I had the opportunity to travel abroad with my youth group on short trips abroad to share my faith. It was during this time I saw God provide not only for me but for those I ministered to. I wasn't the greatest at raising support for these expensive trips, but somehow God made it possible. On these trips accidents happened, unexpected obstacles popped up, and even a terrible storm or two, yet God protected and brought us through it all. I saw my faith grow leaps and bounds during my high school career, and felt beyond confident that I was being called to ministry. It wasn't long before I saw myself studying youth ministry and started considering attending bible college.

Despite how God was working in my life through church, I really wasn't looked at as anyone of note in my high school. I got along fine with just about everyone in school but gaining popularity or having a packed social calendar were never a priority. I had my small circle of friends and was content, that is, until that fateful day I joined the high school business club. There was nothing wrong with the club itself, but more of who I let myself become while a part of it. The club was full of classmates who had bright futures in business, and many went on to great things. Myself, I was merely there because the teacher saw I was a good public speaker and loved to debate. She needed someone to compete in the marketing division for upcoming competitive events and I was a great candidate.

Though I had a small modicum of success in the club and competitions, I did however begin to envy the career and life aspirations of my fellow members. Hearing about classmates getting into Harvard University or the University of Pennsylvania made me begin to question my own path. A path that up until fall of senior year, I would have been adamant had been laid out before me, by God himself. I was going to graduate high school, attend a renowned bible college, and then enter the missions field or start my own youth ministry. Now, sitting in the back of business class I began to doubt all of that. Questioning the wisdom of spending $60,000 per year to attend an out-of-state bible college to obtain a ministry job that would likely not pay much. My peers were gaining scholarships and looking at six-figure salaries or advanced careers on their horizon, I didn't know too many missionaries that were making that kind of money. So, sometime in the spring of my senior year I began to think why can't I make some money and just do ministry on the side. I could get a well-paying job, and then during the summers or maybe a weekend here or there I could go on a missions trip or volunteer at church.

Fast forward a few years, and I find myself in my junior year at the University of Pittsburgh, studying Communications and Psychology with a grand plan to go into marketing and eventually become filthy rich. It all sounded great, but in reality I was miserable. My first year of college was a blur, but the red flags began to pop up during my sophomore year. I couldn't find interest in any of my classes, and my major would change from semester to semester, but I pushed through because I had come so far and my mom seemed so proud. Junior year, however, hit like a ton of bricks. Class sizes shrank, no longer allowing you to hide in the back and avoid participation. The work lasted longer and became more involved, and by this time I had hoped my passion would have taken over and help see me through the late nights in the library and the marathon paper writing sessions. In truth, it was the exact opposite. I had no desire to do anything with what I was learning let alone sit through the difficult classes teaching it.

The tide began to change the spring semester of my junior year. College being as expensive as it was, I could no longer afford it on the lone job I had selling shoes at the mall. I was offered a part-time position at church setting up and helping run the youth ministry.

From the outset I began to look forward to my 10 hours a week at church. I began spending time during lectures planning ice breaker games for the big event nights, and brainstorming themes for upcoming lock-ins while walking between classes.

The final nail in the coffin of my collegiate career at Pitt was when I was offered a chance to be a part of a missions trip to Europe. It was as if my excitement and passion had found me again, and I didn't want give it up this time. So, I finished up my junior year at Pitt, joined the church staff full-time that summer and never looked back. Two years later, I was enrolled at Moody Bible Institute in Chicago, studying youth ministry while also preparing to spend time in the missions field. The joy I felt putting myself back in ministry was indescrlbable.

It's only looking back with several years of hindsight and a bible degree under my belt that I can see the errors of my ways back in high school. I still think about those Wednesday nights spent on the blue tarp as a kid, memorizing verses while learning about God and his plan for our lives. If I had truly trusted God with ALL my heart, rather than doubting his provision when it came to my salary and career path, I may never have strayed from my passion for ministry. I can clearly see how I so often leaned on my own understanding of what college I was supposed to attend and what profession to study, rather than following the gifts and opportunities God had given me to reach and pour into others. Finally, I've also learned the value of acknowledging God in all I do, as there is no clearer way to confirm your calling than to be able to find a profession that uses your God-given gifts to bring glory to His name.

This lesson was a was a hard, time-consuming, and albeit expensive one to learn, but invaluable at the same time. I often keep it active and in the back of my mind, to ensure I never repeat these same mistakes. In the years since I've seen my calling move from missions, to youth ministry, and now into a job field, where surprisingly God still has me pouring into young people as I help them develop their careers in the tech world. It's funny to look back on my life and see where I am now. I wish I could just go back and tell my high school self to be patient, to trust in what God had set before me and to truly embrace God's word in Proverbs 3:5-6. Thankfully I believe in a God who makes all things work for my good. I am now uniquely qualified for the new path he continues to lay before me. He has taken my past stubbornness and turned it into a determination to do his will. From here on out, it is my prayer that He keeps the verse I learned to sing at a young age always on the tip of my tongue, and continue to learn from it.

18

Imperfect Masterpiece
Phillip Michael Williams I
Memphis, TN

My name Is Phillip Williams, but most who know me call me P Mic. I am a singer-songwriter, a father, a teacher, a husband, a church boy, a friend, and mentor to young minds. I am a creative, and like most art, I am an Imperfect Masterpiece. I have been through hell, and experienced heaven on earth in many ways. My story is complicated, but the final product is inspiring and beautiful.

I have always heard that we go through what we go through, not for us personally, but to help those coming up behind us who may be dealing with the same or similar situations. There is so much to share about where God brought me from, that I do not know where to start.

Often, I feel like a little boy standing hands raised reaching for a father that was never there. I was born in 1986 to Alma Jean and Kenneth Williams. That, being one of the few times I've heard of my parents being together. Shortly after my birth, they divorced, and from then on it was just my mother and me. It's important for me to say that because it puts a lot of this story and testimony into perspective. Though I have several siblings, I am the only one born to my mother and father, and I am the youngest on both sides of the family. I was raised around people in church, but I grew up by alone.

I never had the relationship I wanted with my father. I often compared my relationship with my father to Will Smith's character, especially during that pivotal scene in the Fresh Prince of Bel-Aire where Will finally realized his father would never be there for him the way Will needed him to be. I may have had a few weekends with him, here or there, but I grew up as a fatherless child. My father died in 1996, and any hopes of me having a strong relationship with a man-figure died with him.

I became hostile towards God. For most of my life, I had an ingrown disdain and anger towards God for taking my favorite person from me. Little did I know, the person I favored the most, even more than God, never wanted me alive. My father asked my mother to have me aborted and gave her the funds to do so. But thank God she made the choice to keep me and do her best to raise me right.

My mother worked two to three jobs sometimes just to make sure we had everything we needed and ensured that I never knew struggle or lack. Shortly after my father died, while my mother was working, the people she trusted me with showed me more than anyone at any age should have had to experience. From age nine to age eleven I was molested by several men and one woman that I looked up to. People I had known my whole life introduced me to something that sent me on a spiral down a slippery slope. And, because I hadn't been raised with brothers, cousins, or male family members I thought to myself, "There is nothing wrong with this, it's just what guys do when they are alone." Little did I know that what was being done to me would shift the way I saw life.

The way I saw men or males in general was distorted, perverted and altered forever. All the while projecting the good, Pentecostal COGIC (Church of God in Christ) kid, I was expected to be. I battled internally because what was preached in church was contradicted when the stage lights went off. The people who were supposed to look out for me, or so I thought, told me after my father died that I would be dead, in jail or gay by the time I turned twenty. I made up in my mind that I would be everything they said about me. God wouldn't let the first two happen. I couldn't get in trouble with the law for any reason. Even trying to run with the wrong crowd, I was always given mercy, while everyone else I ran with ended up with community service, or with a record. Somehow, I was always protected and shielded. God was trying to show me that I didn't have to go through what everyone else did to find love, affection or attention. My mother prayed and sought out men to help me grow into who God created me to be, but it never worked.

No mentor ever stuck around, no pastor, godfather, friend, family member, or teacher was able and equipped to handle Phillip Michael Williams. I walked around with an overwhelming feeling of loneliness, emptiness, and void. Wanting to replace the father that I never really had, I remembered those words, "By the time you turn twenty you will be dead, in jail, or gay." I had always known from what I experienced as a child, that maybe the only way to fill the void was to accept the fact that I had a same sex attraction, although I believed it was a sin.

I did not ask to be exposed to this life by the different guys or that one woman. It shaped my teenage years and was the thorn in my flesh like Paul described in 1 Corinthians 12. No matter how hard I prayed, and cried, or got "delivered," the desire never went away. I wasn't ready to tell the world, my friends, my mom, or anyone. So, I hid behind the microphone and thought if I sang hard enough, or pushed enough, that people would see beyond my differences and I could blend in.

Fighting so hard to protect myself from myself, I joined groups and choirs filled with people who had my same struggle, thinking I could find strength. However, when "birds of a feather flock together," you just get further into what you want to get away from. One night, on my way to a performance in Colorado Springs, under the guise that I wanted ample energy, I tried to kill myself. I took five Trazadone pills, three Vicodin, three five-hour energy drinks, and two Gatorade drinks, hopped in my car in the snow, hoping that I wouldn't make it to my destination. I believed the world would be better off without a closeted nothing, that couldn't even accept who he was. Leaving no note to my mother, just her empty pill bottles on my bed, I was ready to give up everything and burn in Hell because God couldn't love a sinner like me. By the grace of God, I made it to my destination and threw up, to find out that not one pill had even broken down in my system. God spared my life because I have a story to tell.

I didn't know at the time that I would be in Tampa, FL on senior pastoral staff of a church sitting in the sound booth with a teen who was contemplating suicide because he didn't want to accept the fact that he had a same sex attraction. I was able to share my story with him and show him that he had a reason to live. I didn't know that even though I had given up on love, God had aleady created the woman who would change my life around. The woman who would love me beyond my past and my faults. The woman who would trust me with her past, her present and her future. Though I still battle with the thorn in my flesh, my wife is there to pray me through and even at our lowest points, she's shown me what love is. She allows me to love her beyond what we have both endured and has helped to erase the hurts of our lives before each other.

I didn't know that when I moved from Denver to Tampa in 2007, I would be the one who had to release my mother from life when she was on her death bed in 2010. I didn't know that life would get harder before it got better and that I would find myself homeless and getting kicked out of school because I was sleeping in an abandoned classroom. Nor did I realize that at that same time I would find myself performing and singing in Israel and Jerusalem with people who would become family and love me back to life. I didn't know and I wouldn't have chosen this life. Even though I went through phases of questioning if He loved me or even cared, God was with me through it all.

I didn't know that I would come face to face with several of the people who fast-forwarded my life at an early age and no longer feel hatred toward them. I didn't know my heart would heal and that I could have a relationship with God that was genuine and complete. For this, I am grateful. I'm grateful that even though I struggle, God has used my lowest moments to create a work of art that touches the lives of others daily. Though I am a work in progress, God has shown me the best of him. I didn't die and I am here to encourage someone to live, beyond what you see. Beyond what you feel. You can make it!

19

All Things Work Together
Sonny Kelly, PhD
Fayetteville, NC

For the past two years I have been walking out the eternal truth that "all things work together for the good to those who love God and are called according to His purpose" (Romans 8:28). I have been traveling the nation to share my story about the pervasive and persistent impact of racism in America. In a season of particularly strident strife, where most Americans find it difficult – if not impossible – to discuss race with each other, I have been called to be a peacemaker. I am a believer in Christ who is also a scholar, a teacher, a communicator, an actor, and a playwright. Today, I lead people through uncomfortable, but necessary conversations around race, difference, commonalities, and connection. From corporate conferences to military training sessions, I have seen a hunger for reconciliation and conversation around this nation; and I have answered the call with workshops, performances, and community rap sessions that seem to heal broken hearts of all hues. I was made for such a time as this. But, just a few years ago, I wouldn't have believed you if you told me that I was.

In 2015, I found myself depressed and overworked as I served as the Director of Operations for a struggling non-profit organization in Fayetteville, North Carolina. I did my job well, but it never seemed to be enough. Our revenues always seemed to slump, and we always seemed to struggle just to serve the neighbors in need that depended on us for emergency food, educational resources, home repairs, and youth programs. Employee turnover was chronic and unusually high, and this weighed on my heart. I have always been a peace maker and an encourager. But, in that season, I felt that I was failing at both. Back in 2008, I had achieved my Masters degree in Communication, with the goal of becoming a college professor. My father was a high school teacher, and I'd been acting since I was a child growing up in Southern California. I could feel my heart pulling me to teach, speak, and perform, but my current position seemed worlds away from these paths.

As a means of self-care, I would moonlight as an actor with local community theaters. As a youth pastor at a very small church, I was able to teach Sunday school and children's church lessons. But, I knew there was more. I hungered for more. I wondered why I was plagued with this perpetual fog of fatigue and discontent. Meanwhile, my wife and two sons longed for more of my energy and attention. We had also been caring for our teen-age niece who had a world of trauma and past neglect to digest and process, in addition to acute learning challenges. I felt like I was never quite good enough,

available enough, capable enough to fulfill my purpose in life –
whatever that was.

That same year, I had been in communication with some
new friends that I'd met in the theater world. They were pursuing their
PhD's in Communication and Performance Studies at UNC Chapel
Hill. They opened my mind to the prospect of a new, enlivened,
purpose-filled life. Here was my opportunity to combine my love of
teaching, performing, and engaging with people. However, I learned
that a PhD at UNC Chapel Hill was more than a mere notion. I would
have to take the GRE (Graduate Readiness Exam – a rigorous four
hour standardized test to measure your readiness for post-graduate
studies), apply to the program, and prepare to be a full-time, on-
campus student at one of the nation's premier universities. On top of
all of this, Chapel Hill, NC is about two hours from where my family
lives in Fayetteville, NC. The stipend for a graduate student was
about half of what I was getting paid at the non-profit, and I would
have to somehow pay for an apartment in Chapel Hill and gas for all
of the travel. In addition to these external obstacles, I was beset by a
number of overwhelming self-inquiries: Was I ready for school again?
Could I make this time commitment? Would my family survive
financially and emotionally? Was I smart enough?

Well, I thank God for a strong, faithful, faith-filled wife. One
day, after watching me wallow in self-doubt and self-pity, my wife
Elenah urged me, "Why don't you just apply? Take the GRE and
apply. The worst they can do is say 'No." If they do, then you have an
answer from God." To make a long story short, I took her advice. I
visited the campus and met some of the professors and graduate

students in the Communication Department, and I fell in love with the place. You might say that I felt it in my "sha-na-na" that God had called me to this place. But, how would we make ends meet? How would we keep our family together? As a leap of faith, I applied and we asked God to do the rest.

In the spring of 2015, I was admitted to the Graduate School of Communication at UNC Chapel Hill! I would start my five year journey to a PhD in the Fall of 2015. Shortly thereafter, my wife landed a government job, in addition to her Air Force Reserve position, that paid more than I was making at the non-profit. I also learned that I had won a fellowship that would boost my stipend during my first year of study. The G.I. Bill would pay for my lodging and living expenses at school. My wife and I knew that right then and there, we were in the center of God's will! As, I've heard it said before, "Where God gives vision, he also gives provision."

While God provided, He certainly did not make things easy. Within my first year of school, our teen niece, whom we had adopted by then, was clearly not happy. She confessed to us that she was confused her about her sexuality and that she didn't feel that she fit in our household. She became defiant at home and at school. She was failing her classes and the strife between my wife and her became unbearable. We loved her so deeply, but it seemed that she just couldn't receive it. Meanwhile, I was away at school for four to five days a week, completing three years of course work. My wife was holding it down with three kids as a single working mother most of the week. I felt so helpless.

The coursework was a bear! I had never had to read so much with such close attention to detail, nuance, and substance. I slept very little and struggled to prepare for every class session. Meanwhile, most of my colleagues were ten to fifteen years younger than me (I was 39 when I started the program). These youthful minds had seen all of the latest research in the field. They were so smart and well spoken. I was overtaken by what they call "imposter syndrome." That is to say that I heard this constant internal voice that questioned my intelligence, capability, and, even my purpose!

I thank God for my wife's prayers and encouragement. I suggested that I quit school on more than one occasion; and on more than one occasion, she demanded that I press into my purpose. She refused to let me quit. Through many tears, I prayed more, read more, and focused on the gifts that I brought to this new space. I was a veteran, a father, an actor, a playwright, and a man on a mission. Within two years, I started to find a groove. I shared my joy and my faith with my colleagues and professors. While I didn't always have the right answers, and my lack of experience with the subject matter was clear, they could not deny this indomitable spirit that drove me.

Inspired by the work and teaching of my advisor Dr. Renée Alexander Craft, I designed a critical performance ethnography project that would address the challenges experienced by Black youth in America. By my first summer, I began to do my research with a youth program that was part of the non-profit that I used to work for in Fayetteville. It was a project that my collaborators and I called "My Life Matters." Armed with my deeper theoretical understanding of communication and performance studies, I launched an ongoing self-expression workshop that helped a group of 35 troubled teens to find their voices and to express themselves through poetry, rap, and storytelling. By the time the summer was over, twelve of the kids performed their work live for an audience of fifty adult community members, one of them being the Mayor! Later, the Mayor invited three of the middle school girls to sing their inspirational song and tell their personal stories at the opening of a City Council meeting. After the performance, the girls' faces lit up to know that what they had to say mattered to adults in their community. One of them beamed when she told me, "I feel like I can fly!" My God! In that moment, I knew exactly why He had put me onto this path!

But, that wasn't all. In addition to empowering youth, God had called me to be a peacemaker. The work that I do now around racial reconciliation, equity, and inclusion, was born of a painful conversation that I had with my then seven-year-old son Sterling back in April of 2015. On our way to school, my son and I listened to a radio report about riots in the streets of West Baltimore, MD, in the wake of Freddie Gray's death. Freddie Gray was an unarmed Black man who was killed while in police custody. All my life, I had seen the bodies of Black people disproportionately arrested, demeaned, and destroyed by people with power and pistols. As I heard the radio report about Freddie Gray, visions of the lynchings of Emmett Till and Trayvon Martin swirled through my head.

Looking into my back seat, I beheld a beautiful Black boy, who would one day grow up to be a Black man - a Black man, who would look an awful lot like the pictures I had seen on the news of the now deceased Freddie Gray. I realized then that it was time to have a father-son "talk" about identity and survival. How do you explain to a child the fact that he faces a world that often condones and enacts violence against bodies that specifically look like his? So, I had what many parents of Black children in America refer to as "The Talk," with my son. I warned him that racism could attack his heart, mind, or body at any time. I challenged him to be better, smarter, and more aware than those around him. All the while, I lamented the fact that, given the wrong situation, in the wrong time and place, none of this advice could insure his complete protection from the slings and arrows of racism.

It took me a week or two after having this short, awkward conversation with Sterling to feel the anguish that it caused me. After an appointment in downtown Fayetteville, I found myself walking the streets on a sunny day – my mind racing – tears streaming down my face - my fingers feverishly typing, groping for the thoughts, feelings and words that went through me on that day. The result was "Sterling's Story" – an 8 to 10-minute personal story about my love for my son and the despair that I felt in having to inform him that he lived in a world where some people – important people who wield the power to harm him – would not value his life as I did.

Since that spring day in 2015, I have worked the story over and over in my head. I have shared it at storytelling festivals and other performance venues, as part of my personal repertoire. When I learned that "Sterling's Story" was part of a larger phenomenon known as "The Talk," I knew that I had to do more with this story. I knew that it could begin to humanize the racialized politics of issues like "stop and frisk," "zero tolerance" school policies, and the "Cradle to Prison Pipeline." After taking a class on developing original performances with Professor Joseph Megel at UNC Chapel Hill, I was compelled to transform "Sterling's Story" from a short story into a theatrical experience – one that has emerged as more experience than performance. So, over the course of three years, I wrote a one-man play called The Talk. It began as a cathartic place where I gave voice to the anguish I uncovered when I reminisced upon that painful conversation. In my research, I have found that this piece doesn't just tell my story – it gives words to an anguish that parents of color, and especially parents of Black boys, endure around this country.

The Talk is a one-man performance that draws on the voices of ancestors, elders, youths, and intellectuals to engage in the difficult conversations that we must have with our children as we prepare them to survive and thrive in a racialized America. In this original 80-minute performance, I raise the voices of over 20 people and call audience into deep reflection and inspired action regarding racial division, marginalization, and violence in the U.S. This eclectic theatrical experience weaves together interactive theater, a dynamic embodied performance, and a multi-media production with the words of James Baldwin, Langston Hughes, W.E.B. DuBois, Howard L. Craft, Ta-Nehisi Coates and others.

I incorporated this project into my PhD work and developed a dissertation entitled Pipelines to Pathways: Reframing and Reclaiming Black Youth Identities through Performance. I continued to work with the youth in Fayetteville through the "My Life Matters" project during the summers of 2017 and 2018. I put The Talk on stage and performed this one-man show for packed houses in 2018 and 2019. All the while, I finished my coursework, completed my comprehensive exams and wrote my dissertation. I learned that when you are driven by purpose, what seems impossible is only one more step on the pathway to God's calling.

I successfully defended my dissertation in March of 2020 and, today, my one-man performance of The Talk has been seen by thousands of people across the country. I have used the performance to engage diverse audience in difficult conversations around race, difference, and how we can better honor the dignity of Black youth in America. At its core, The Talk is really about a father's profoundly abiding love for his son. With this work, I invite audience members into a complicated, but loving, space where we are all encouraged to imagine new possibilities together.

Today, I am a full-time instructor of Communication at Fayetteville Technical Community College, where I educate, encourage, and empower students to use their voices for good. I am continually invited to perform The Talk and to lead workshops around communication, theater, performance, racial reconciliation, equity, and inclusion around the nation. My wife is now at the top of her career field, and I am in a position to support her as she pursues her dreams. My sons Sterling and Langston are now 12 and 9, and they are thriving in their school work, artistry, and social development. My niece Danielle just turned 21. She returned to live with my mother in California at the age of 17, and went on to complete her high school degree and find employment. I don't know how He did it, but God stretched our resources, time, and energy to not only make it through a harrowing season, but to come out victorious on many fronts! I don't know that I would have consciously chosen this path for myself. But, I can tell you that there is no place I'd rather be. All things have truly worked together for my good and I am determined to continue to press forward toward the mark that God has set for me!

Sonny Kelly resides in Fayetteville, NC. He can be reached at sonnykelly2000@yahoo.com. Learn more about Sonny's life work and purpose at www.sonnykelly.com.

Author's Note

"… it wasn't as easy as I thought it would be. But I appreciated the moments of reflection. Thank you for thinking of me." – *Be Encouraged by Black Men* contributor

"I appreciate the opportunity. It was some therapy I didn't realize I needed forreal." – *Be Encouraged by Black Men* contributor

----

If this book has done nothing else - it has already done enough. This book was yet another one of my God ideas.

2020 has been a year for the books! One pandemic after another, and forced time at home prompted me to really be intentional with how I was spending my time. I needed an outlet. The continued murders of Black men were really heavy on my heart and I wanted to center their voices using resources that I had easy access to; my faith in God, and the ability to produce another published book. Thus, the idea for *Be Encouraged by Black Men* was birthed.

At a time when being Black, particularly a Black man, is frightening, discouraging, and filled with defeat I wanted to provide an additional narrative. I wanted to provide the perspective of God's grace and mercy via these men of melanin. I wanted to remind folks by centering the voices of black men specifically, that God can do exceedingly abundantly more than we can think, feel, dream, or see.

Social media and news outlets reminds us that Black men are dispensable. I want to remind you that these same Black men are husbands, fathers, business owners, sons, brothers, mentors, friends, and children of God. They are loved (1 John 3:1). They are redeemed (Ephesians 1:7). They are set apart (Romans 8:30-39). They are made with purpose (1 Peter 2:9).

Working on this book was a true pleasure. I've come to experience God through the vulnerability of 19 Black men! I am grateful to each and every Black man who even considered my ask of sharing their testimonies.

You all have supported my dreams in ways that I can't explain.

While working on this collection, I have laughed, cried, jumped for joy, and even wondered why God would allow one to experience some of the things that these Black men have endured. However, at the end of every single chapter I was shaking my head, lips pursed, and taken aback .....literally relishing at just how good God is.

I was raised by a Black Man.
I am married to a Black Man.
I am assisting to raise Black Man.

It is my sincerest hope, that through this project, you were Encouraged by at least one, Black Man.

#BlackLivesMatter
#DontTryBlackMenTryGod
#BeEncouraged

-Jerrica Stovall

ABOUT THE AUTHOR

Jerrica Stovall is a native of Virginia Beach, VA, but currently resides in St. Petersburg, FL with her husband and daughter where she works in Higher Education. Additionally, she has a bonus son who lives in South Carolina. She is a second time author who is excited about the continued potential of her projects. She is a woman of her faith, a new found fitness fiend, a juicer by day - Trader Joes inspired chef by night, a lover of reading, and is always exploring new places to go via Yelp.